Advance Praise for Timothy Gallagher's
Discerning the Will of God

"When we are doing the will of God, that alone is enough to satisfy us. When we are not, all the pleasure and possession of the world are not. How many books have you read on the subject of discerning God's will? Whether it is one or a hundred, you should read this book." — **Matthew Kelly,** *New York Times* bestselling author of *The Rhythm of Life* and *The Dream Manager*

"*Discerning the Will of God* is the sixth and perhaps most important in Fr. Timothy Gallagher's books on discernment. It raises the perennial question for the committed Christian: How can I really know God's will for me? Gallagher addresses this through what has become his hallmark style, namely the interaction of an Ignatian text — here, the three times in which a sound and good choice may be made — with practical examples. The result is a work of far-reaching significance in the hope it inspires that God's will may be known, embraced, and lovingly fulfilled."
— **Gill K. Goulding, C.J.,** University of Toronto

"The teaching of Ignatius Loyola on discerning the will of God is his most important contribution to Christian spirituality. It is also extremely difficult to explain. One approach is to present and comment on the relevant parts of the Spiritual Exercises. Another is to work with examples taken from the actual experience of people today. The strength of Gallagher's new book is that he combines the two approaches in a lucid and helpful way. What I most admire is what lies behind Gallagher's book — an extraordinary patience in gathering so many apposite examples. These come in part from his own experience as a spiritual director and in part from his reading. This patience reveals a great love of people who struggle to find the will of God in the complexities of today's world. It also manifests an appreciation of the ministry of spiritual direction and the place that it holds in facilitating Christian decision making."
— **Brian O'L**eary, S.J., Milltown Institute of ology

Discerning
the **Will** of
God

Discerning
the **Will** of
God

An Ignatian Guide to
Christian Decision Making

TIMOTHY M. GALLAGHER, O.M.V.

A Crossroad Book
The Crossroad Publishing Company
New York

The Crossroad Publishing Company

www.crossroadpublishing.com

Printed in the United States of America.

The text of this book is set in 12/18 Sabon. The display face is Tiepolo.

Library of Congress Cataloging-in-Publication Data
Gallagher, Timothy M.
    Discerning the will of God : an Ignatian guide to Christian decision making / Timothy M. Gallagher.
    p. cm.
    Includes bibliographical references.
    ISBN-13: 978-0-8245-2489-0 (alk. paper)
    ISBN-10: 0-8245-2489-6 (alk. paper)
    1. Decision making – Religious aspects – Catholic Church. 2. Discernment (Christian theology) 3. Ignatius, of Loyola, Saint, 1491–1556. Exercitia spiritualia. 4. Spiritual life – Catholic Church. 5. God – Will. I. Title.
    BV4509.5.G345 2009
    248.4 – dc22

This printing February 2017

Contents

Part Two
DISCERNMENT

Part Three
FRUIT

Acknowledgments

I am deeply grateful to the many people whose generosity made the writing of this book possible: once more, to Joseph Schner, S.J., the Jesuit community of Pedro Arrupe House, and the faculty and staff of Regis College, Toronto, who again offered me warm hospitality and continuing support during a time of writing; to Claire-Marie Hart for her unfailing assistance and expert editing; to Carol McGinness for her generous aid with permissions to quote copyrighted material; and to William Brown, my provincial, for his personal encouragement and for providing a further time of writing.

I am also profoundly grateful to those who accompanied me with their counsel prior to the writing and their reflections on the manuscript during the writing itself: George Aschenbrenner, S.J., Harvey Egan, S.J., James Gallagher, Theresa Galvan, C.N.D., Fr. Paul Gitter, Gill Goulding, C.J., Carol Lankford, Gertrude Mahoney, S.N.D., and Edward O'Flaherty, S.J. Their support and insights were a treasured resource during the preparation for and writing of this book.

I express my warm thanks, too, to John Jones, Editorial Director of the Crossroad Publishing Company, and, with him, the staff at Crossroad; working together on this and the earlier books has been a consistently positive and fruitful experience.

Finally, I thank the following for permission to reprint copyrighted material:

Excerpts from the *New American Bible with Revised New Testament and Revised Psalms* © 1991, 1986, 1970 Confraternity of Christian Doctrine, Washington, D.C., used by permission of the copyright owner. All Rights Reserved. No part of the *New American Bible* may be reproduced in any form without permission in writing from the copyright owner.

The Catholic Edition of the Revised Standard Version of the Bible, copyright 1965, 1966 by the Division of Christian Education of the National Council of the Churches of Christ in the United States of America. Used by permission. All rights reserved.

Excerpts from Robert Baram, ed., *Spiritual Journeys: Twenty-seven Men and Women Share Their Faith Experiences.* Copyright © 1988 Daughters of St. Paul, Boston. Used with permission. All Rights Reserved.

Excerpts from *Priest Vocation Stories*, FAITH Publishing Service, Diocese of Lansing, Mich. © Catholic Diocese of Lansing. Used with permission.

Excerpts from Timothy M. Gallagher, O.M.V., *Meditation and Contemplation: An Ignatian Guide to Praying with Scripture.* Used with the permission of the Crossroad Publishing Company.

Excerpts from *Moving in the Spirit: Becoming a Contemplative in Action*, by Richard J. Hauser, S.J., Copyright © 1986 by Richard J. Hauser, S.J., Paulist Press, Inc., New York and Mahwah, N.J. Reprinted by permission of Paulist Press, Inc. *www.paulistpress.com.*

Excerpts from Christine Mugridge and Jerry Usher, eds., *Called by Name: The Inspiring Stories of 12 Men Who Became Catholic Priests* (West Chester, Pa.: Ascension Press, 2008). Used with permission.

Excerpts from *The Selected Poetry of Jessica Powers*, published by ICS Publications, Washington, D.C. All copyrights, Carmelite Monastery, Pewaukee, Wisc. Selections from "Letter of Departure," p. 43, and "The Place of Splendor," p. 123. Used with permission.

Excerpts from Michael Scanlan, T.O.R., with James Manney, *What Does God Want? A Practical Guide to Making Decisions.* The permission to reproduce copyrighted material for use was extended by Our Sunday Visitor, 200 Noll Plaza, Huntington, IN 46750, (800) 348-2440. Website: *www.osv.com.* No other use of this material is authorized.

Excerpts from Jules Toner, S.J., *Discerning God's Will: Ignatius of Loyola's Teaching on Christian Decision Making.* Used with permission: copyright © The Institute of Jesuit Sources, St. Louis. All rights reserved.

Excerpts from *Vocation in Black and White: Dominican Contemplative Nuns Tell How God Called Them.* Copyright © 2008 by Association of the Monasteries of Nuns of the Order of Preachers of the United States of America. Used with permission.

Introduction

When Faced with a
Major Life Choice

The muted sound of traffic outside was the only accompaniment as I walked through the church. The morning sun shone dimly through the stained-glass windows. I was alone in the quiet church.

I reached the head of the aisle and stood for a moment before the altar. In that moment, I felt these words arise from deep within my heart: "We are not leaving this place."

The church and residence were old and in need of repair. My religious community, entrusted with both, had either to renovate both or relocate. Much depended upon this decision. Renovation would involve great demands upon our limited personnel and finances. It would require changes in the lives of several priests and so affect the many people they served. Relocation would involve relinquishing long-established ministries. And, as provincial superior, the decision was mine.

For a year I had studied the question, held meetings, gathered information, and sought the advice of competent persons. I knew the issues. I had prayed, asking, "What is your will, Lord? What do you want us to do? Do you want us to stay? To move? Help me in my indecision. Help me to see." Months were passing. A decision was necessary — and still I could not decide.

1

In that moment before the altar, an answer simply arose in my heart: "We are not leaving this place." I sensed that God wanted us to stay, wanted us to accept the challenge of renovation, wanted the necessary changes, wanted the new life that renovation would bring, and wanted me to begin the process right away. For several minutes I stood before the altar, deeply stirred.

As I remember that moment now, many questions arise in my heart. For a year I had sought God's will: Why had I been unable to find it? Had I not tried hard enough? Not prayed enough? Was I seeking God's will the wrong way? Had God in fact responded, but I hadn't recognized that response? Was it God's design that the search would continue throughout that year? If so, why?

And how was I to understand that moment before the altar? Was that truly God's voice? Was it the gift, in a moment, of an answer? Could I follow that answer with confidence? Could I be sure, as I began changes affecting many lives, that I was truly doing God's will? Or did the words "We are not leaving this place" arise more from my own need than from God? From my love for a church in which I had ministered for years? From the growing pressure to act?

I see similar questions in the lives of others every day, in their own situations.

A man is unhappy in his work and considers starting his own business. He knows that this will involve risk for himself, his wife, and his children. He loves God and wants to do God's will. He wonders: "Do you, Lord, will that I take this step? Or do you want me to continue in my present job?" How will he find his answer?

Financial concerns suggest to a woman that she should move to another area. Her teenage daughter enthusiastically urges a certain place where several friends live. The woman understands her daughter's desire but is concerned about the neighborhood and the school there. This woman, too, loves God and desires to do God's will. She, too, wonders: "Lord, do you will that I say yes to my daughter?"

A professionally successful young man has returned to the Church and is growing in prayer. For the first time, the thought of priesthood arises in his heart. The thought both appeals to him and troubles him. He has always assumed that he will marry and have children. In fact, he and the young woman he is dating have already spoken of marriage. Now he is confused. He, too, desires to do God's will but is unsure of how to find it.

A similar situation occurs in the life of a young woman. She feels a deep attraction to religious life as a sister and is seriously exploring this call. Then she meets a young man who clearly wishes to marry her. He respects her love for religious life, however, and waits to see what she will decide. Now, for the first time, she is unsure. Might she be mistaken about her call to religious life? Is it possible that God is calling her to marriage instead? Months pass, and still she has no answer. How will this woman find God's will?

This is a book about such questions. In my own life, and
in thirty years of retreat work and spiritual direction, these
questions arise continually: they are questions about *discerning God's will*. This book explores how we can discern God's
will in such situations: when persons of faith, who love God and
want to do God's will, are faced with choices between options
that are good in themselves. These include:

• this career or that,

• one's present job or a new job,

• work or further studies,

• a change of place for the family or no change,

• involvement in this ministry or that,

• marriage to this person or to another or not at all,

• marriage or priesthood,

• marriage or religious life, and so forth.

In such situations, how can these persons *discern God's will?*
How can they find a clarity that will permit them to pursue
wholeheartedly the course chosen, confident of doing God's
will? In many years of working with discernment, I have heard
this question repeatedly. More than any other, this question
awakens the desire for a clear teaching about discernment. I
have written this book in response to that desire.

Our guide in this exploration will be St. Ignatius of Loyola.
The central focus of his Spiritual Exercises is precisely the
situation just described. With unparalleled mastery and prac-
ticality, St. Ignatius provides a way of "seeking and finding the

divine will" (*SpirEx*, 1) — of discerning God's will — in choices between good options.

I am deeply grateful to St. Ignatius for his teaching on discerning God's will. That teaching offers me clarity in times like that morning in the church and in many similar situations. It prepares me to seek God's will when the options are all good and the choice is left to me. In retreats and spiritual direction, I have seen St. Ignatius's teaching resolve doubt and release energy for service in people who love God. This teaching is a gift for all in the Church, in all walks of life, whether priest, religious, or layperson, single or married. My purpose in this book is to offer a clear, essential, and usable understanding of Ignatius's teaching on discernment to those who must make choices, and to their spiritual guides.[1]

In earlier writing on discernment, I discussed Ignatius's teaching on the *discernment of spirits*.[2] This book explores Ignatius's related but distinct teaching on *discernment of God's will*. *Discernment of spirits* answers the question: How may you understand the spiritual movements in your heart (consolation and desolation) with their related thoughts (of the good spirit, or of the enemy), and how may you most fruitfully respond to them? *Discernment of God's will* answers the question: How may you know what God wills you to do in this choice you face? As will become apparent in chapter 6, the two overlap at one significant point, but they are not identical.[3] A complete treatment of Ignatian discernment, therefore, requires the present book.

This is a practical book. Ignatius's teaching is rooted in experience — his own, and that of those he served. That teaching,

consequently, is clearest and most helpful when presented in its
original setting: the spiritual experience of persons who seek
God's will. For this reason I present Ignatius's teaching on discernment primarily through the experience of persons who have
sought and found God's will.

I have found some of these experiences in written sources.
Most, however, I quote from personal interviews with persons
who shared experiences of seeking God's will and gave their
explicit permission to cite their words in this book.[4] I have
done so with careful respect for confidentiality. Thus I refer
to them without names ("a man says," "a woman says") or
with names other than their own. For the same purpose, I
have, at times, altered the external details of their stories. In
each case, however, the account I give faithfully reproduces the
spiritual experience described by these persons. Every experience recounted in this book — including the scenarios briefly
sketched above — is taken from real life.

These persons represent all walks in life. Some are religious,
some priests. Many are laypersons, married or single. All share
a love for God and the desire to do God's will. I am deeply grateful to them: without their stories, this book would not have been
possible. Through their stories, our discussion of discernment
will be rooted in the full richness of lived experience.

And I am grateful to them in a personal way as well. I
knew that the writing of this book would involve simultane-
ous study of Ignatian sources and personal interviews. What I
could not have foreseen, however, was the interaction between
the two. Often, as I pondered some aspect of Ignatius's teaching, an interview would illustrate that teaching in concrete

experience. The convergence of teaching with experience was powerful. I learned in a new way that Ignatius, in his teaching on discernment, simply articulates what occurs when a person who loves God seeks "the divine will" in situations like those described. Once these persons and their guides have learned Ignatius's teaching, they will understand their own experience with increasing clarity — and so increasingly find the "divine will" they seek.

This book presents St. Ignatius's teaching on discernment found in the Spiritual Exercises. In the first part, I discuss *preparation* for discerning God's will: why doing God's will matters, the disposition of heart that best allows us to seek God's will, and the spiritual means toward gaining that disposition. In the second part, I explore *discernment* itself: the three different ways in which God answers the questions raised above. In the third part, I consider the *fruit* of discernment: the growth discernment brings, and the joy of living in God's will.

At times in the interviews the persons speaking and I would both find ourselves deeply moved. Most often this would occur at the end of the conversation when, through sharing stories of search and, at times, of struggle, we would sense how God's provident love had guided the many steps of the process. As I begin this book, I approach discernment of God's will with reverence for the endlessly creative mystery of God's work in human hearts. I approach it, too, with gratitude for Ignatius's teaching, a gift of the Spirit to the Church, which offers those who seek a path toward discernment. This is the gift we will now explore.

Text of St. Ignatius

Three Times in Which
a Sound and Good Choice May Be Made*

The first time is when God Our Lord so moves and attracts the will that, without doubting or being able to doubt, the devout soul follows what is shown to it, as St. Paul and St. Matthew did in following Christ our Lord.

The second time is when sufficient clarity and understanding is received through experience of consolations and desolations, and through experience of discernment of different spirits.

The third time is one of tranquility, when one considers first for what purpose man is born — that is, to praise God our Lord and save his soul — and, desiring this, chooses as a means to this end some life or state within the bounds of the Church, so that he may be helped in the service of his Lord and the salvation of his soul. I said a "tranquil time," that is, when the soul is not agitated by different spirits, and uses its natural powers freely and tranquilly.

---

*SpirEx, 175–77. Author's translation, following the original Spanish. For Ignatius's complete text (*SpirEx*, 175–88), and for a note on the translation, see the Appendix.

PART ONE

PREPARATION

Chapter One

The Question

Which Choice Does God Want?

Here where we walk the fire-strafed road and thirst
for the great face of love, the blinding vision,
our wills grow steadfast in the heart's decision
to keep the first commandment always first.

— Jessica Powers

ROBERT knew that he faced a decision. He had finished his degree and was teaching in college. "That year," he says, "I realized that I needed to make a decision about my vocation."
Robert explains:

My family always had a love and reverence for the priesthood. My uncle was a priest. He was a great guy, a kind of wisdom figure for me. It was a privilege to serve Mass for him when I was growing up. I remember watching priests when I was in grade school and thinking, "That would be great to do." But I didn't really think much about it.

When I went to college, I started going to daily Mass. That was where the idea of a vocation started to be stirred. I went to daily Mass all year. I was also making visits to the Blessed Sacrament. That was where I first felt deep,

deep stirrings in my heart; I really started feeling the pull. I would spend an hour before the Blessed Sacrament in the evening, absorbed in peace and serenity. I said to myself, "Whatever this is, I want it. If it means being a priest, I'll do it."

But there was a struggle in my heart because since high school I also did a lot of partying — too much drinking and some drugs. It got better, but it was still a struggle sometimes. I also wondered if I could live celibately.

Then matters took a new turn for Robert:

In my sophomore year in college, I started dating Helen. I really learned from her what it means to love. I was in love with her and she with me. She blew my horizons into eternity. I could see endless possibilities in life with Helen. All that stuff about being in love and self-sacrifice — I would have given my life for her. Sometimes she would be in the chapel too when I was praying in the evening, and I would say, "Lord, the love I have for you and for Helen are the same thing."

There was intense intimacy, but it was a very chaste love. In my junior year we talked about marriage. Then I started to get scared. The intimacy was intense, and I thought that if she really found out about me — the partying, the drinking, all of that — she wouldn't want me.

At the same time, when I was dating Helen, the idea of priesthood became solid for me, real and consistent. Several persons asked me if I'd ever thought of being a priest.

One day I had lunch with the priest who was the chaplain. I really liked him. He was real, and he seemed happy. He told me that he thought I would make a good priest and that I should consider the priesthood. For the first time this became real, and I started to get scared. So I told Helen that we needed just to be friends. It was very hard. She knew I was thinking of the priesthood.

Robert's hesitation continued:

I finished my degree and started teaching. Once I was talking with a friend who told me that I needed to do something, that I'd been on this marriage-priesthood seesaw for two or three years. I said to myself, "Yes, he's right. It's time for me to face this question."

What should Robert do? Are the "deep, deep stirrings" and the "pull" his heart experiences toward priesthood indications that God is calling him to be a priest? Does the deep and chaste love he experiences for Helen, the "endless possibilities" in life he senses in her company, signify that God is calling him to marriage? What is God's will for Robert? How may Robert *discern* in this choice?

MONICA has been growing in her life of faith. After six years of emptiness, far from God, she returned to the Church. She lives a faithful life of the sacraments, has a spiritual director, and prays daily. She describes a moment of decision in her family:

I got a call that my father was terminally ill. I went to see him. The day I arrived he was in the hospital; I realized that

I had come at the right moment. For two weeks I visited him regularly. A lot of the family was there. My sisters and I began to discuss what we should do: should we bring him home or find a good nursing home for him? I didn't know what God wanted me to do.

In a very different setting, similar questions arise. Monica, like Robert, loves God and wants to do God's will. What is God's will in this situation? How will Monica find clarity?

BRIAN describes yet another situation of decision. Early in his marriage, his wife Lisa's deep faith brought him close to the Lord. He recalls:

We had been married for several years, and our third child had just been born. I had worked in finance for a number of years, but found myself increasingly interested in serving in a more direct way. The thought of becoming a doctor continued to arise in my mind, all the more as my life of faith deepened. I spoke with Lisa about this. We both thought that I could do it, but it would mean some real sacrifices for Lisa while I was in medical school. For several months we talked and prayed about this.

Again, the same questions arise. Again, people who love the Lord and seek the Lord's will search for a way to discern that will.

When the choice is between a good and an evil option — to be honest or dishonest in my business dealings; to be faithful to my marriage vow or priestly ordination or religious consecration, or not; to speak the truth or a lie — God's will is evident:

God never wills us to choose what is evil or would signify infidelity to definitive vocational commitments.[1] Something similar may be said of choices concerning responsibilities inherent in a state of life already chosen: parents who must choose between proper care of their children or additional voluntary activities, no matter how good; a pastor who must choose between the needs of his parish or other ministries that require prolonged absences, and so forth. God, who calls us to a state of life, also calls us to the tasks inherent in that state.

Robert, Monica, and Brian, however, face a different kind of choice. Robert must discern between two options, both of which are good: marriage or priesthood. And his choice regards precisely his state of life: he is free to choose either. Monica and Brian also face choices which the criteria just named do not resolve: Does God will that Monica care for her father at home or with the aid of a well-equipped institution? Does God will that Brian remain in finance or enter medicine?

This is the question Ignatius addresses in his Spiritual Exercises, the question that is the focus of this book: When people who love God and want to do God's will face choices between options *all of which are good* and that *they are free to choose,* how can they discern God's will?[2] Ignatius's first step is to lay the foundation for a reply. In our next chapter, we will explore that foundation.

Chapter Two

The Foundation

God's Infinite Love and Our Response

*I am created to do something or to be something for which
no one else is created; I have a place in God's counsels, in
God's world, which no one else has.... God knows me and
calls me by my name.* — John Henry Newman

"We Love Because He First Loved Us"

"We love because he first loved us." This biblical verse (1 John
4:19) lays the foundation for every search for God's will: when
the human heart discovers that this world is not empty, that its
life is not meaningless, that it has been loved from all time, that
its very existence is a gift of love, then that heart rejoices and a
yearning to respond awakens. Then the *human will* thirsts for
that *communion* with the *divine will,* which is mutual love —
the love for which we are made, and which, as Augustine says,
alone gives rest to our restless hearts.

MICHAEL describes the moment when he discovered this foundational truth for himself:

I can actually point to a moment when the pieces of my
fragmented life came together for the first time. I was a

18

sophomore in college, going in several directions at once, trying to keep my options open, plagued, in particular, with questions about God. On the day of my nineteenth birthday I went into the woods on the outskirts of town and grandly announced to God, "I'm staying here in the woods until you do it."

What was "it"? To let me know for sure that he existed. To reveal how I could know him. To speak to me.

I stayed in the woods all day and into the evening. I was hungry and thirsty, and it was getting cold. I was a little scared, but I was stubborn. I was determined to stay in the woods until I got an answer.

The answer came at around 8:30 in the evening. The puzzle of God suddenly cleared up in my mind. A conviction grew in me that he did indeed exist and that the Church was indeed an institution that told the truth about him. I could have confidence in it. The Lord spoke to my heart too. He loved me. He would forgive my sins and heal my wounds. I was home. All this was a free gift of God. I was a desperate case, so he had pity on me and gave me everything at once.

This was the foundation. The vocation I discerned later flowed from this relationship with the Lord that began that evening in the woods. That was the key. The relationship has been there ever since.[1]

Yes, this is the foundation: he loves me, he will forgive my sins, he will heal my wounds; I am home. This "free gift of God" awakens the heart's longing to respond: a heart that knows itself

so loved longs to live in *relationship with God.* And, as Michael
says, all discernment flows from this relationship with the Lord.

JACK had abandoned his practice of faith for seventeen years.
He recounts his experience:

> One evening...while working late, I went to his [a col-
> league's] engineering library to find the address of the
> Tennessee Valley Authority, U.S.A. I had ideas of acquir-
> ing American civil engineering experience. Instead I found
> a book of Catholic sociology on his shelf...entitled *The
> Framework of a Christian State.* In it were three lines which
> changed my life and still affect it profoundly. They said,
> in effect, that man has within himself a certain nature
> which he must discover. From that nature spring certain
> rights he can enjoy (right to a good name, to private
> property, to an education, to marriage, etc.) and certain
> duties which he must carry out (duties to respect those
> same rights in others, who are cast in the same mold).
> The word "discover" rocked me. It implied the opposite of
> being a "self-made man." It revealed to me that there were
> many "givens" that I did *not* have to struggle for — iden-
> tity, dignity, origin, gifts, destiny — all given me *already* by
> something or someONE else — but *not* me. I could also
> see that my task was to seek and discover these "givens"
> within; unwrap them, appropriate their richness...and
> share them with others.... WHAT a discovery![2]

Jack too has discovered the foundation, the God-given truth of
our identity, dignity, origin, personal gifts, and destiny.[3] His heart

stirs with enthusiasm, and a search begins: "I could . . . see that my task was to seek and discover these "givens" within; unwrap them, appropriate their richness . . . and share them with others." At the heart of his search is the thrill of discovery of Someone whose love has bestowed this dignity and destiny upon him.

CATHERINE had finished college and had begun working. She was dating a young man and was also considering religious life. Months passed, and her search for God's will continued. One day she was driving home from work. Catherine describes what occurred that evening:

> The presence of Jesus palpably filled that white '93 Ford Escort *LX*. I hesitate to describe the experience for fear of making it sound more or less than it was. It was like being in a room with someone you love but cannot see; yet, you can feel his eyes on you. He didn't say anything. He just looked at me. . . . And his look: it was like when a guy looks at you, not with lust, but with a desire that you be his girl. . . . It's astounding to have God look at you like that, both exhilarating and humbling because you know it's totally unmerited. To my surprise, I felt very much like when I had first fallen in love, except it was magnified a hundred times.
>
> A very direct dialogue ensued.
>
> I kept saying, "What do you want? What do you want?"
>
> The gist of his reply was, "You can do whatever you please. You can get married; you can have the job of your choice; but it would please me if you have me."
>
> I melted.

He had asked a question and waited for an answer. He wouldn't force me. It was powerful, but gentle persuasion. Never have I felt so free yet, at the same time, it seemed impossible that I should say no. I pulled into the parking lot and sat in my car, finally saying, "Whatever. Whatever you want, Lord." Then the presence that had surrounded me seemed to pierce through me and close around my heart.[4]

We stand on holy ground. Catherine's narrative again expresses foundational truths: once again, awareness of the gift of love, and of relationship with God; once again, the desire to respond to this sensitive, gentle, and infinite love that fills the human heart: "What do you want? What do you want?" Catherine senses God's profound reverence for her human freedom: "I have never felt so free." And her heart opens in love to the Love she experiences: "Whatever you want, Lord." The profound truths of the *foundation* are all contained in this grace-filled narrative. Those who build their lives upon this foundation long for *communion of wills* with God — they long to do God's will.

In yet another setting, **CHRISTOPHER** too makes this foundational discovery:

I grew up without any knowledge of Christianity and without any real faith. When I was nineteen, I joined the military. I was very confused about many things, certainly about God and religion. When I was in the military, I kept meeting a priest who was there, and he impressed me. I saw how he lived and how he prayed, and it had a big effect on me. Whatever he had, I wanted. For the first time I began to realize that religion is serious. This priest gave me a rosary and said that I should pray it. I resisted; that was passé, something my grandmother did. Then one of the others said to me: When you're on duty all night and have nothing else to do, why not pray? So I started to pray the rosary. A priest explained to me how to pray it, and so I just did it, day after day.

Then one time I had a powerful experience while praying the rosary. It was like waves coming over me — I knew that I felt the presence of God. Now I knew that God existed, because he had touched me. And I thought: if God exists, then I want to be a priest.[5] This was my vision at the time — it reflects how little I started out with when I began to turn to God. I spoke with a priest I knew, and he said: "Easy, easy. Calm down. Discernment takes time."

About a year later, a group of us spent an evening with a group of women students who were visiting in the area. When I walked in, I saw only one. I was immediately smitten by this one girl. I made it clear that I would sit next to her in the restaurant. On the way back, I told the others that I had just met my wife.

Now a struggle begins for Christopher:

Then I became confused. I thought that I was betraying my decision to follow God in the priesthood, that maybe I was just following my body's wishes. I talked to the priest, and he said to bring this into prayer. I was afraid to do it. I thought God would say: "I want you alone. I don't want you to have this woman." So I didn't want to pray about this.

Finally, I became so distraught that I had to do something about it, and I did pray about it. To my surprise, from my prayer I got a feeling — an emotion, not words — of being a child in his mother's arms. I got this feeling of security. I would get this strongly when I started to pray. I got a feeling of peace, that it's okay, go ahead with this relationship. I had the sense that God was pleased with this.

In spite of the distance, she and I were able to meet again. My heart was overflowing with love and happiness about this. The more I prayed, the happier I became.

Christopher reflects on what had changed:

My experience of God in my prayer contradicted my image of God. I had thought of God as demanding and jealous. I thought that a vocation was like my commander in the military: he doesn't take your wants into consideration, but just says, "You do this!" I saw that God was not like my commander, that God made me, that he made me to be happy, that this was what he had made me for. I learned this from what I experienced in my prayer.

Once more, the foundation is here: the discovery of faith, joy-filled encounter with God, continuing relationship with God, and desire to respond to God. As Christopher grows in knowledge of God, he, like Catherine, experiences the joy of freely responding to God—the joy of doing God's will.

"To Do Your Will Is My Delight"

"To do your will is my delight." These words of Psalm 40 express the deep desire of Jesus' heart: *to do the will of the Father* by whom he knows himself loved (John 5:20; Heb. 10:5–10). They also express the deepest desire of every human heart rooted in the foundational truths described. When Michael experiences this foundation that evening in the woods, a process of discerning God's will begins. When Jack discovers the God-given gift of his origin, identity, and destiny, his heart too delights, and he begins a search for God's will. When Catherine grasps the depth of God's reverent and infinite love for her, her heart cries out, "Whatever you want." And when Christopher experiences the truth about God, he too is set free to pursue God's will.

PETER recounts his dawning awareness of this guiding truth:

I also realized at a very young age, obscurely but strongly, that the truth about God had to be far simpler than I had been taught, as well as far more complex and mysterious. I remember surprising my father with this realization (which was certainly because of God's grace rather than my intelligence, for I was only about eight, I think): "Dad, everything we learn in church and everything in the Bible comes down to just one thing, doesn't it? There's only one thing we have to worry about, isn't there?" "Why, no, I don't see that. There are many things. What do you mean?" "I mean that all God wants us to do — all the time — is to ask him what he wants us to do, and then do it. That covers everything, doesn't it? Instead of asking ourselves, ask God." Surprised, my father replied, "You know, you're right."

In college years, Peter understood this truth with new depth:

One summer, on the beach . . . I read St. John of the Cross. I did not understand much of it, but I knew, with undeniable certainty, that here was reality, something as massive and positive as a mountain range. I felt as if I had just come out of a small, comfortable cave, in which I had lived all my life, and found that there was an unsuspected world outside of incredible dimensions. Above all, the dimensions were those of holiness, goodness, purity of heart, obedience to the first and greatest commandment, willing God's will, the one absolute I had discovered, at the age of eight.[6]

With great clarity, Peter perceives "the one absolute" in the life of faith: to will God's will. He summarizes with simplicity and profundity the whole of discernment: All God wants us to do is to ask him what he wants us to do, and then do it. On this foundation, a solid life of faith may be built.

STEVEN and LAURA reflect on the discernment that led to their marriage. When asked how consciously this was a discernment *of God's will* for their lives, Steven replies: "Totally. We wouldn't have had it any other way." Laura agrees, and explains:

We were in college in the late eighties, and we didn't speak that language then. At that time, in that context, we wouldn't have used the language of vocation and discernment. We would have spoken of "mission," of "desire," of "something more going on," or, most likely, of "ministry." There was definitely a call to ministry in it. We knew that this marriage was of God.

In the preparation for marriage, when we chose the readings, we chose Luke 5:1–11 as the Gospel — Peter called by Jesus to lower the nets. We clearly had this sense for our marriage, that we were called by Jesus and sent as a married couple.

This is a powerful and beautiful image of marriage: a man and woman called and sent by Jesus. Steven and Laura consciously approach marriage as a response to God's will in their lives. In Peter's words, they *will God's will* and make this the "one absolute" in their lives.

PATRICIA describes one of the steps that led to her marriage to Anthony:

> I went through a huge discernment process, asking God if this was the right person. No one ever told me about different vocations: marriage, religious life, and priesthood. But I always sensed that it was God's will for me to be married and have children. One day, driving in my car, I asked the Lord: "Is Anthony the one you want me to marry?" I sensed God saying yes. This moment was one step in the process.

Patricia's process of discernment is guided by one desire: *to do God's will.* For this reason, she undertakes a discernment process; she asks God if Anthony is "the right person," that

is, the one *God wants* her to marry; she opens her heart to
marriage and children because she senses that this is God's will
for her. Her question in the car reflects this same search for
God's will: "Is Anthony the one *you want* me to marry?"

JEREMY tells of a decision he faced in his career:

> I was doing well in my job, but, after about five years, some
> struggles within the company made me wonder whether I
> might need to seek another job. My wife and I talked about
> this, and she was very supportive. For the next three years
> we thought and prayed about this, and we watched the
> situation develop in the company. We wanted to be sure
> that we did what God wanted. We weren't looking just for
> what was comfortable; we wanted what God wanted. Every
> day during those years I would pray, "Lord, help me to
> know and to do what you want me to do."
>
> Through the way things developed, through prayer, and
> through talking it over with my wife and my spiritual direc-
> tor, I came to see clearly that God wanted me to seek a new
> job. When I saw this clearly, I felt a profound sense of joy
> and peace. I had an image of the way God called Abra-
> ham to leave his country with his family (Genesis 12). It
> felt something like that, a new step for me and my family,
> but I knew exactly what God wanted us to do.

In this choice, Jeremy and his wife consistently seek one
thing — God's will: "we wanted what God wanted." Jeremy
expresses this desire in a daily prayer of the heart: "Lord,
help me to know and to do *what you want me to do*." When

Jeremy sees God's will clearly, he experiences joy, and is ready to respond without reservation.

Peter, Steven and Laura, Patricia, and Jeremy now have the foundation on which discernment can be built: they have experienced God's love and desire to respond in communion of will with God — they seek, above all else, to do God's will. All discernment must be built upon this foundation.

In a famous meditation, John Henry Newman writes: "God has created me to do him some definite service; he has committed some work to me which he has not committed to another. *I have my mission.*"[7] In the Scriptures, the Lord says to Jeremiah: "Before I formed you in the womb I knew you, before you were born I dedicated you, a prophet to the nations I appointed you" (Jer. 1:5). Isaiah describes a similar consciousness in the Servant of the Lord: "The Lord called me from birth, from my mother's womb he gave me my name" (Isa. 49:1). Paul, too, knows that his mission is from God, "who from my mother's womb had set me apart and called me through his grace" (Gal. 1:15). This awareness, however, is exemplified above all in Jesus who, when coming into the world, said, "Behold, I come to do your will, O God" (Heb. 10:7). Jesus has come "to do . . . the will of him who sent me" (John 6:38) and always does "what is pleasing to him" (John 8:29).

Awareness that God has created us out of love and ceaselessly offers that love to us;

a consequent thirst for communion of wills with the one who so deeply loves us;

the consciousness that each of us can say with John Henry
Newman, "He has committed some work to me
which He has not committed to another,"

the desire to live like Jesus who always did the will of the
One who sent him:

this is the *foundation* of discernment.

In our next chapter, we will explore the dispositions of heart
that permit us to build solidly upon this foundation.

Chapter Three

The Disposition
Openness to Whatever God Wills

One night when Blessed Peter Pettinaio of the Third Order was praying in the cathedral of Siena, he saw Our Lord Jesus Christ enter the church, followed by a great throng of saints. And each time Christ raised his foot, the form of his foot remained imprinted on the ground. And all the saints tried as hard as they could to place their feet in the traces of his footsteps, but none of them was able to do so perfectly. Then St. Francis came in and set his feet right in the footsteps of Jesus Christ.
> — From an early Franciscan text

"Whatever You Want, Lord"

When **CATHERINE** encounters the love of God, she replies from her heart, "Whatever you want, Lord." Her words express complete openness to God. We sense that Catherine, in the grace of this moment, need only know what God wills for her and she will unhesitatingly say yes. She describes this moment in these simple and striking words: "Never have I felt so *free*" — free to hear whatever God will say to her, free from all that might

31

limit her readiness to respond, free to say yes wholeheartedly to God's will. This, Ignatius tells us, is the *disposition of heart* which best permits us to discern God's will.[1]

JOHN recounts a Christmas Day prayer:

> During my senior year of high school, after Christmas din-
> ner, I went back to our parish church and knelt in front of
> the manger and thanked God for all he had given me — my
> life, my wonderful family, my excellent education — and
> I said to Jesus that I wanted to give it all back to him. I
> thought I was being generous, but it was God who was
> being generous with me.[2]

John, too, as he prays, is blessed with the gift of freedom. Conscious of God's providential love in his life, he desires to be completely available to God in response. We sense that when John in fact understands what God wills, he will readily embrace that will. John's heart, too, is *disposed* for discernment.

MATTHEW is a religious priest ordained for ten years. In a retreat a few years earlier, he first felt a desire for further studies in theology. He explored this possibility in prayer and in spiritual direction. Finally, he spoke with his religious superior, who encouraged him to contact the provincial, the one who would decide. Matthew wrote to the provincial, who invited him to meet. Matthew continues:

> I got to the provincial's residence a few minutes early, and
> he was delayed some minutes, so I sat alone in the parlor

for about twenty minutes. I was feeling some anxiety, and so, while I waited, I prayed. I thought back to the retreat in which this interest first awakened and realized once again that this didn't come from me. As I prayed, a deep peace came into my heart. Whatever would happen, I just wanted to say yes. I was there only because I'd been saying yes to what I'd been hearing in prayer, and that was all I wanted to do. I just wanted to say yes.

There was great freedom in that prayer in the provincial's parlor. This whole matter was not coming from me. Whatever the provincial would say, yes or no, would be fine. This was not coming from me.

"Whatever would happen, I just wanted to say yes": this, too, is a heart *disposed* to discern the will of God. Conscious that, in this decision, God's will is mediated to him through his provincial superior, Matthew is completely open. We may note that for Matthew, as for Catherine and John, the gift of this disposition is given in prayer. For Matthew, as for them, it is accompanied by a great sense of peace.

This openness to God, without which discernment cannot be made, cannot be taken for granted. In fact, in his Spiritual Exercises, Ignatius prepares us for discernment primarily through the quest for this openness. Through various spiritual means, we seek from God the grace of such openness.[3] Two examples, one involving a call to marriage and the other a call to religious life, will suggest something of what may be involved in this quest.

MICHELLE shares her story:

I grew up without any attractive model of faith. The idea that God had a purpose for me just wasn't there. It was up to me to make what I wanted out of my life.

Then, in college, I went through a time of great pain and darkness. In the midst of it, I met a group of students who loved the Lord and were athletic, fun to be with. Meeting them was the beginning of my conversion.

During that time, one day when things were very dark, I read Jesus' words in the Gospel: "Come to me, all you who labor and are burdened, and I will give you rest" (Matt. 11:28). I saw myself laying the burdens of my heart at his feet, at the Cross. I sensed Jesus saying to me: "You can give this to me, and I give you your identity as a child of God." I had the sense that there was not just a comfort in this, but a call. And I said yes.

In the following years I continued to grow in my faith. I learned a lot about it, and I learned about a personal relationship with the Lord. That was when my prayer life began, and I came to know the Lord. He spoke to me in a way I'd never known before.

The question of vocation now becomes central for Michelle:

Then I met a woman who asked me if I had discerned my vocation. This was the first time I'd ever asked the Lord about this. I had always assumed that he wanted me to get married. Now I asked, "What do you want, Lord?"

I visited one religious community but knew it was not for me. I thought about another but didn't feel attracted to it. I began to get frustrated. I was convinced I was called to be a religious and was doing my best to respond, but the Lord wasn't showing me what he wanted. I started to doubt myself, wondering if in some way that I wasn't seeing I was the cause of the problem. Finally I did try a religious community but after a short time knew that it wasn't right, so I didn't stay.

The time of healing approaches:

I went home again and began working. I knew that I needed a community, and so I joined a Catholic young adult group. That was where I met Scott. He was a lot of fun. He started courting me, but I was cautious. After trying the religious community, I still wanted to keep my heart open. So there was a lot of hesitancy.

Then I made an Ignatian retreat. During that retreat many questions came up. It was the most personal encounter I'd ever had with the Lord. I experienced the Lord as healer. My relationship with the Father was there during the whole retreat. He took me through the years of pain. It was an amazing experience of his hand on my heart, so close to me. I felt awe that he knows me so deeply, that he is so gentle, so loving.

One day after Communion, the question came: Will you allow yourself to love Scott? I talked with the director about it and prayed a lot about it. There were other times of consolation about Scott in my prayer.

The day after the retreat was a day of feeling so filled with the Lord that I didn't want anything, not to eat, any-thing. I brought this to the director and realized that God was showing me that *he* was the one who would fill me, above and beyond this thing I'd become fixated on — my vocation, struggling so hard to find *a* vocation: religious life or marriage.

That day was filled with consolation and a wonderful confidence that whatever the vocation, God was the one who would fill me through it. I had felt that my only access to God was my vocation, and so I was desperate to find it. I went back home, able to relax and to be in the relationship.

And then the final step:

I'd never felt this much peace in my vocation before. Still, there was some fear, asking whether I could really rest in this. It took another retreat to finally overcome this. I had to go back to the Father's arms and face that part of me that doesn't trust my heart. On the retreat the Lord revealed to me how Scott's love for me had been healing of my ability to receive God's love for me. I am absolutely in awe of Scott's unconditional love for me, and it frees me to receive God's love: it frees me to be who God has always wanted me to be.

So it was not a desperate "Lord, let me know that this is my vocation!" but a receiving of this gift as it unfolded. When Scott proposed, it was easy to respond.

Once more we stand on holy ground. God, by a rich outpouring of healing love, leads Michelle to the freedom that permits her to discern: "it *frees* me to receive God's love: it frees me *to be who God has always wanted me to be*." For several years

Michelle tries diligently — even desperately — to discern God's will.[4] The "amazing experience" on retreat of God's great love frees her to *receive* the *gift* of her vocation from God: "So it was not a desperate 'Lord, let me know that this is my vocation!' but a receiving this gift as it unfolded." Once this healing occurs, the *disposition* of heart that permits discernment is present, and the discernment itself soon follows: "When Scott proposed, it was easy to respond."

The second experience suggests further issues that may arise in the quest for this disposition. RICHARD reflects on his vocational discernment:

I was aware of two conflicting desires. First, I had the desire to go to college, become a lawyer, raise a good Christian family, and continue to enjoy the type of life I had known. This was my dominant desire. But I also experienced another desire: to join the Jesuits. I had a very happy experience in my Jesuit high school. I was attracted to many aspects of the Jesuit life, and I could see myself joining the Jesuits and helping high school students in much the same way they had helped me. There were, however, aspects of this life that were not attractive to me, such as poverty[5] and the lack of a family. My problem during the second half of my senior year was to decide which of these two desires was from God. At this time in my life I did not make a formalized reflection. As I look back now, however, I can see how much of my thinking was conditioned by the forces that were playing upon me. My cultural conditioning surely

pointed me toward getting a college education, becoming
a successful professional, and enjoying Christian family
life. This was what almost one hundred percent of my
classmates would be doing.

Richard continues:

> I recall praying intensely . . . to know God's will; I also recall
> vigorously putting the idea of joining the Jesuits out of my
> mind whenever it occurred and turning my attention to
> going to college and getting married. I was not open to
> God's will at that point, nor did I have any intent to carry it
> out should it be made known to me. . . . As I reflect on it now,
> I can see clearly that the necessary conditions for seeking
> God's will were not present: I wanted to know God's will
> only if it confirmed my initial inclination toward going to
> college and getting married.[6]

Richard, as he reviews the discernment that led to his Jesuit
vocation, remembers praying intensely to know God's will.
Clearly, even at this early stage in his discernment, Richard
knows God's love and desires to respond. Nonetheless, he
recalls that, at this point, the necessary *disposition* for discernment was not present: "*I was not open* to God's will at that
point. . . . *The necessary conditions for seeking God's will were
not present.* . . . I wanted to know God's will *only if it confirmed
my initial inclination.* . . . " The necessary conditions to which
Richard refers are precisely the openness and freedom that *dispose* Catherine, John, Matthew, and Michelle (after her healing)
to say yes unreservedly to God's will:

"Whatever you want, Lord."

"I said to Jesus that I wanted to give it all back to him."

"Whatever the provincial would say, yes or no, would be fine."

"When Scott proposed, it was easy to respond."

How do we reach this graced disposition of heart? Few questions in discernment are more crucial than this, for all else in our effort to discern depends upon this disposition. Its absence, as in Michelle's and Richard's first attempts to discern, blocks the road to discernment. Its presence, as in the other examples cited and in Michelle's and Richard's later discernment, opens the door to discernment. Having described this disposition, Ignatius turns immediately to the quest to attain it.[7]

"Loved to the Death by Jesus Christ"

DEBORAH narrates the events that began her discernment:

I was always a Catholic, but Church was not an important part of my life growing up. There were serious problems with alcohol in my family, and I got into this, too. In business, I was very successful and became a vice-president in the large company I worked for. In those years I had no relationship with God. At that time, God was a punishing God for me.

One evening I went to a relative's wake. There were hundreds of people there, and I felt an overwhelming sense of love in that room. I found a copy of the Serenity Prayer there and began praying it daily.

Then things got to a desperate point with alcohol and my whole life. I knew I had to make a choice. I went to the parish church and sat in the back. I said to God, "I can't do this alone. I need your help." I never drank again after that day. Every day for six months after that, I would go to the church and ask God's help.

One Sunday I reached the lowest moment of my life, feeling completely alone. After Mass I saw a flyer in church about a retreat. I called and went on the retreat. It was there that I had my major reversion to the Church. The retreat infused me with knowledge of right and wrong. I learned that God loved me, that I could have a relationship with God. But, above all, I saw that my life was going the wrong way morally. All that I cared about now was that God loved me. And I knew that I had a mission in life which had to do with life — giving life and helping life in others.

I am deeply grateful to Deborah for the honest sharing of her story. The power of God's grace enters Deborah's isolation and suffering and leads to new life. Her courageous decision to reject alcohol, followed by her turning to God in the retreat, frees her to encounter God no longer in fear but in truth: "I learned *that God loved me,* that I could have a relationship with God....All that I cared about now was *that God loved me.*"

Knowing that she is loved (the foundation), Deborah can review her life with new openness: "I saw that my life was going the wrong way morally." We sense that there is no longer any fear in this — God is no longer the punishing God of her earlier years — but rather a new freedom to change. The experience of God's saving love awakens in Deborah a desire for moral newness: to overcome sin and the pain it causes. *In that moment,* a sense of mission is born in Deborah — a quest for discernment of God's will begins: "And I knew that I had a mission in life." Deborah's account richly reveals a key experience in attaining the disposition for discernment: the experience of ourselves as *loved sinners,* loved in our failures, faults, woundedness, and pain — loved in a way that frees us to seek moral newness and so creates a heart ready to discern.[8]

DAVID describes the troubled beginnings of his years of discernment:

> When I was in college I began dating a girl. I dated her for four years, and we had a sexual relationship. The whole time I was conflicted. There was the excitement of being accepted by a woman, of being loved, the adventure of the time spent together. The conflict arose through the sexual part. There was something good in the relationship, but my conscience was always troubled. I never cut myself off from the Church and Mass. There was a search going on in me. I was deep into the mystery of woman and deep into the mystery of the Mass. The inauthenticity of the juxtaposition of the two was tearing me apart. There was always a tension in the relationship.

Clearly, in such circumstances discernment will be difficult if not impossible. The difference in disposition between, for example, Catherine's wholehearted "Whatever you want, Lord" and David's conflicted and divided heart is evident. If he is to discern, David must first overcome the obstacle that binds his freedom. Like Deborah, he must turn to God and seek courage to change what he knows is "inauthentic" (morally indefensible) in his life. In fact, with some struggle, David does terminate the relationship and begins a profound search for God's will. Once he, too, experiences himself as *loved into freedom from sin,* a path to discernment opens. His discernment eventually leads to a Christ-centered and blessed marriage.

WILLIAM recounts the early stages of his discernment:

I was a party animal during college. It was funny though. Once in a while I would think about the priesthood. My friends told me to have a beer. Back then, if someone had told me I would be a priest...I would have found that completely unbelievable.

Later on, I went to graduate school to work on a Ph.D. in biochemistry. During my second year, I had what I now call a religious conversion. At the time, I had no idea what to call it. All I knew is that God became very real for me. Prayer became very important. Scriptures were alive and were filled with God's word that spoke to me. The Blessed Mother became very real as well. Before too long I was involved in the Church. The youth minister and others from the parish spoke to me about the priesthood and gave me some books to read.

I had a huge struggle going on inside me because the idea of the priesthood was no longer just a distant idea.

Now it was coming to the surface as a possible life choice.
I was very nervous about it. I was on a different path, but I
wanted to be open to what God wanted for me. Each day I
would try to make at least a holy hour to pray for help.[9]

In less dramatic circumstances than David's, the same dynamic
of renewal is present. William's discernment begins through *a
change of life,* which he describes as a "religious conversion."
The center shifts in his life as unbridled partying gives way
to spiritual searching: "God became very real for me." Prayer,
Scripture, a daily holy hour, and involvement in the Church
free his heart to hear the question of discernment: "the idea of
the priesthood was no longer just a distant idea." Through this
change of life, the disposition for discernment has emerged: "I
wanted to be open to *what God wanted for me.*"

Deborah, David, and William, in their individual circumstances, undergo a spiritual change that sets them morally
free and opens the path to discernment. This opening of the
human heart to the Savior's healing love — to freedom from
the burden of sin — is the first key step, Ignatius tells us, in
preparing for discernment.[10] As sin weighs less and less on the
heart, the freedom to say "Whatever you want, Lord" grows
correspondingly.

An experience in the context of the Spiritual Exercises themselves will confirm this point. THOMAS describes this gift of
grace:

The first week of the *Spiritual Exercises* focuses on the need for
the sinner to approach Jesus Christ with a thoroughly honest

examination of life. . . . I dreaded to admit my responsibility, fearing God's rejection of me. However, because St. Ignatius instructed retreatants to take their sinfulness to Jesus Christ on the cross, I learned that he died precisely to forgive these sins.

What amazed me was that the more honest I could be before our Lord in confessing my sins, the greater peace I felt. No longer was "Jesus loves sinners" simply words. This was a powerful experience. . . .

Knowing myself as a sinner who is loved to the death by Jesus Christ gave me a freedom to offer myself to be whatever the Lord wanted me to be. The specific vocation — Jesuit priest or brother, diocesan priest, husband and father of a family, or single layman — no longer mattered because I knew that Christ loved me so much that *anything* he wanted for me would be the best thing for me.[11]

The experience of the love of Jesus for the human heart wounded by sin amazes Thomas. It is powerful and brings him peace. Thomas's experience of himself "as a sinner who is *loved to the death by Jesus Christ*" awakens in him "a *freedom to offer [him]self* to be *whatever the Lord wanted [him] to be*": that is, it awakens in him the *disposition* for discernment.

Deborah, David, William, and Thomas, though they begin in widely diverse spiritual circumstances, are all increasingly becoming persons ready for discernment. In Ignatius's words, they are persons who, in humble and trusting dependence on God's grace, "are going on *intensely purifying their sins* and *rising from good to better* in the service of God our Lord" (*SpirEx*,

315).[12] They have experienced God's love (foundation), seek openness to God's will in response, and are now *going on* — faithfully persevering — in the quest for that purification and growth that best prepare them to discern.

Sent by Jesus

LAURA describes the key weeks in her discernment of marriage:

Steven and I began dating during our junior year in college. This was a crucial time for me. I knew what attraction was, but what happened to us in those weeks was much deeper than attraction. On top of that, I knew what love was. I knew what it meant for a love of someone to touch "forever." But this was more again than that. I knew what it was for two people to look at each other, to love each other, to know that this touches eternity. This was more. It was turned outward. There was something moving through us, out toward other people, that said "forever," but also allowed us to help others become their best selves. I had never experienced that before. It was more than an attraction, with love; it was mission, hospitality. It sent us forth. And because it did, it allowed me to receive even more.

Laura and Steven's discernment of God's will rests on more even than a love that says "forever." Together they experience being *sent* — they experience their calling as a *mission* in service of others. This sense of mission is decisive in their discernment.

ARTHUR, too, understands his vocation as a call to serve:

During college I thought seriously of priesthood and tried attending the seminary when I graduated. After one year I knew it was not for me. I went to dental school, graduated, and started working as a dentist. I was dating at the time and presumed that I would marry.

Then my parents got very ill, and I had to leave the city and take care of them. I was an only child. For many years, they needed all the energy I had outside of work, and when they died, I came to see that God was calling me to the single life. Certainly, I've always struggled to know his will, and I'm sure that this is God's call for me. I'm sure that it has been the right thing to do.

I've always seen it as a life of service. I've always wanted to serve the Church and contribute to it. I've tried to do that in my professional work the way St. Francis de Sales said, to do my work well. I've been a lector in my parish, taught catechism and RCIA,[13] and helped on the parish council for many years. I teach now at a Catholic college, and I've been able to help many students in making decisions about their careers.

Arthur understands his calling as a mission in the Church and in the world, "a life of service."

JOHN speaks of his mission as well. Christ has become the key that defines his life:

I was director of human resources for [a major corporation] about 40 minutes from Manhattan. I was intimately involved in the lives of about 3,500 employees across 35 states. Image, power, and control dominated our lives.

With an undergraduate degree in business administration and a master's in business and labor relations, I went from college right into management. I worked for seventeen years in middle and upper management in the Detroit area and New York, before entering the seminary.

My former self would find it interesting that image, power, and control still dominate my life, but it's the image, power, and control of Christ, the Good Shepherd, that defines me now. The joy and peace that accompanies this "letting go" cannot be adequately described. It can only be experienced (cf. Phil. 4:4–9).[14]

A fundamental shift, centered on Christ, has occurred in John's life. He has "let go" of one vision of image, power, and control, and embraced that of Christ. A joy and a peace that cannot be adequately described accompany this new Christ-centered criterion of life.

For Ignatius, finally, everything in the disposition that permits discernment *centers on Christ:*

the Christ who *loves me to the death* and frees me from sin and woundedness (*SpirEx,* 53);

the Christ who lovingly invites me *to share in his own mission* of saving and healing human hearts, and to make of this mission, in whatever specific calling he gives me — marriage, priesthood, religious life, the single life — the goal of my life (*SpirEx,* 95);

the *humble and poor Christ* who invites me to embrace this same simplicity of heart — the "letting go" of which John speaks — and so be truly free in my discernment (*SpirEx,* 98, 146, 167).

Clearly, then, if we are to discern well, we must come *to know Christ deeply,* personally, intimately, so that *we may love him more* and *follow him more closely* in our choices (*SpirEx,* 104). Ignatius dedicates the largest part of preparation for discernment precisely to this: repeated contemplation of Jesus in the Gospels, so that, our hearts filled with Jesus, we may know, love, and follow him in our discernment.[15]

An early biography of Francis of Assisi offers us a lovely description of a heart utterly centered on Christ. In the text, we read:

The brothers, moreover, who lived with him knew how his daily and continuous talk was of Jesus. . . . Indeed, he was always occupied with Jesus; Jesus he bore in his heart, Jesus in his mouth, Jesus in his ears, Jesus in his eyes, Jesus in his hands, Jesus in the rest of his members. . . . He always bore and preserved *Christ Jesus and him crucified* [1 Cor. 2:2] in his heart with a wonderful love.[16]

A person transformed by Jesus, bearing Jesus in every part of his humanity; a person ever centered on Jesus "with a wonderful love": this is a person *ready to discern.*

Such, then, is the disposition that prepares us to discern
     God's will:
the *foundational awareness* of God's infinite love for you;

the *healing encounter with Jesus* who loves you to the
    death to free you of sin and burden;
and, at the heart of all, the continuing quest for *heartfelt
    knowledge and growing love for Christ.*

How may we grow in this disposition? In our next chapter
we will consider the spiritual means Ignatius offers in reply to
this question.

Chapter Four

The Means

"How she prayed!" he thought. "It was plain that her whole soul was in her prayer. Yes, that is the prayer that moves mountains, and I am sure her prayer will be answered."
— Leo Tolstoy

Spiritual "Exercises"

From the outset, Ignatius describes preparation for discernment as a series of spiritual exercises — spiritual activities that persons undertake in order to "prepare and dispose" themselves to "seek and find the divine will" (*SpirEx*, 1). In this chapter we will focus on those spiritual means that Ignatius offers as *preparation* for discernment. Wise use of these means, he tells us, *disposes* our hearts to discern well.

Holy Eucharist

For Ignatius, the Eucharist is a daily element of the Spiritual Exercises; it is also the daily context of his own practice of discernment.[1] As we have seen, the same is true of **ROBERT'S** discernment:

When I went to college I started going to daily Mass. That was where the idea of a vocation started to be stirred. I went to daily Mass all year. I was also making visits to the Blessed Sacrament. That was where I first felt deep, deep stirrings in my heart; I really started feeling the pull. I would spend an hour before the Blessed Sacrament in the evening, absorbed in peace and serenity.

In this account, as in many others, the Eucharist is the central "means" toward discernment, the place of deep encounter with Christ that awakens the desire to respond: "That was where I first felt deep, deep stirrings in my heart." For Robert, as for many, frequent or daily Mass becomes a key means toward discernment; and for Robert, as for many, prayer before the Blessed Sacrament outside of Mass deepens the process.

A single woman faced with a difficult discernment about work says: "Last spring I made an eight-day Ignatian retreat. Since then I began to make a holy hour every day before the Blessed Sacrament. While I was discerning, I brought this decision daily to the Lord in that hour." A married man recounts his practice while discerning a change in his career: "When I would do the pros and cons, I simply got confused. So I started going to daily Mass. My decision to go to daily Mass was linked to my need for clarity in this decision."

A woman describes the prayer that led to her discernment: "I went to daily Mass. There was something about the Mass that drew me. I used to love to listen to the Scriptures." Another tells of how the Eucharist stirred new longings within her. She had

been away from the Church for some years, and now returned
to Sunday Mass:

> I got up and went to Mass. Nothing dramatic happened at
> the Mass, but I got to thinking, "What am I doing with my
> life?" I was twenty-three at the time. So I started going to
> Mass and helping in the parish. I started teaching religion
> classes for kids, and I went to some parish missions. At
> the hospital, on lunch break, I would go to the chapel and
> would say to God, "What are you asking?"

Here, too, the Eucharist fosters new closeness to Christ and
awakens questions of discernment: "I would go to the chapel
and would say to God, *'What are you asking?'* "

A final witness reveals the *transforming* power of the Eucharist in discernment: "In my visits to the Blessed Sacrament each
night in the lovely college chapel, I begged and begged; but I
noticed my earnest pleadings being transformed into, 'Not my
will but Thine be done.' "[2] Prayer before the Lord in the Blessed
Sacrament gradually awakens the disposition that permits discernment. In fact, this woman reached clarity about God's will
soon after. Clearly, Ignatius's invitation to place the Eucharist
at the heart of discernment bears rich fruit.

Sacred Scripture

For Ignatius, the primary focus of prayer in discernment is
Sacred Scripture and, above all, the life of Christ in the Gospels.[3] Because discernment is a response to Christ (*SpirEx*,

91–98), growing knowledge and love of Christ, above all, prepare us to follow his call (*SpirEx*, 104). Ignatius teaches that
the ideal preparation for discernment is ongoing *contemplation of Christ in the Gospels*. Those who discern will find such
contemplation invaluable.[4]

Some examples will illustrate why Ignatius so warmly rec-
ommends this prayer to those who discern. RICHARD contemplates — that is, shares imaginatively — the encounter of Jesus
with Zacchaeus (Luke 19:1–10). He describes his experience:

I took the place of Zacchaeus. I was there in the tree, waiting for Jesus to pass by. When I imagine the Gospel, I don't
see things in great detail. I just had a sense of being in
the tree, waiting for Jesus to come. Then he did come, and
he stopped. I sensed that, for him, at that moment, I was
all that mattered. He was giving me his entire attention.
And that was where the prayer stopped — Jesus looking at
me, with his whole attention, with warmth, with desire to
be with me, and my looking at him in response. It was
quiet and happy. It lightened my worry and self-doubt.
I knew that Jesus wanted to be with Zacchaeus regard-
less of Zacchaeus's sinfulness, and that by being with him,
simply by letting him know that he was loved, Zacchaeus would be transformed. I felt that Jesus was with me
in the same way. Then I heard Jesus say, "Richard, come
down quickly, for today I must stay at your house." And
we were together in the house, without many words, just
together.[5]

As Richard contemplates this Gospel event, he grows in personal *knowledge* of Christ: "I knew that Jesus wanted to be with Zacchaeus"; "I sensed that, for him, at that moment, I was all that mattered." Through his contemplation, Richard's relationship with and *love* for Christ deepen: "Jesus looking at me, with his whole attention, with warmth, with desire to be with me, and my looking at him in response. It was quiet and happy." Clearly, if Richard heeds Ignatius's invitation and prays regularly in this fashion, his readiness to *follow* Jesus — that is, his readiness to discern — will grow as well.

SUSAN also contemplates Jesus in the Gospel:

> I was praying with Jesus walking on the water [Matt. 14:22–33] at the point where Jesus says to Peter, "Come." I could see what was happening. I could feel the cold and the wind. I was one of those in the boat, sitting there as one of the passengers. I could see that Peter was really scared, and I thought of times when I've been afraid too, wondering what was going to happen to me. And, like Peter, I started shouting out to Jesus too, to save us.[6]

Through her contemplation, Susan personally shares Peter's encounter with Jesus: his response to Jesus' call, "Come," his fear, his cry to Jesus. Peter's experience touches her own — "I thought of times when I've been afraid too" — and leads her to Jesus: "I started shouting out to Jesus too, to save us." As she prays, Susan, like Richard, is growing in her relationship with Jesus. If Susan prays faithfully in this way, her readiness to follow Jesus — her readiness to discern — will grow. Ignatius invites those who would discern to such prayer with Scripture.

Silence

A professional woman in her thirties faces an important choice, one that will affect her career now and that may eventually lead to discernment between marriage and religious life. She describes her struggles early in the process:

> At this point I had no spiritual director. I was getting more and more frustrated — there was so much noise in my soul. When I could, I would stop in a church near work, but that was the only silence I had all day. Otherwise, there was noise all around me all the time. Someone gave me the name of a priest, and I called him. When we met I was in tears, feeling panic-stricken and frustrated. I didn't know what to do. There was so much noise that I couldn't hear God's word.

This woman is not alone. Her words explain why Ignatius prescribes *silence* as the ideal climate of discernment (*SpirEx*, 20): silence that allows us to hear the "still small voice" (1 Kings 19:12) in which God speaks to the human heart.[7]

PATRICIA recounts the beginnings of a discernment that led to marriage:

> My real spiritual journey began in college when I was twenty-one or twenty-two. I realized that I knew very little about my faith, and so I asked to go through RCIA.[8] It was

one of the best things I ever did as an adult to come to
know my faith.

Then I did a Cursillo [retreat] weekend. It was four days.
On that retreat I had my first experience of silence, and I
loved it. It was the first time I had ever experienced silence.
It was a huge thing. I learned about the spiritual life and
about being in a group. I got a spiritual director at this
time — one of the priests who had been on the weekend —
and started meeting.

Patricia rightly perceives her experience of silence as "a huge
thing." It is a new experience for her, and she loves it. Through
it she learns much about the spiritual life and, through it, she
takes further steps for spiritual growth. As she reflects on her
discernment, Patricia recognizes the fruitfulness of silence.

Patricia experiences silence for the first time in a *retreat*.
Evidently, for Ignatius, a retreat is the ideal setting for a discernment of significance. The Spiritual Exercises are precisely
that: a retreat.

We have already encountered many for whom retreats were
grace-filled times in discernment. Michelle attains freedom to
discern through an eight-day Ignatian retreat: "Then I made an
Ignatian retreat. . . . It was the most personal encounter I'd ever
had with the Lord. I experienced the Lord as healer. . . . It was
an amazing experience of [the Father's] hand on my heart, so
close to me." A second Ignatian retreat confirms her healing
and prepares the discernment that follows shortly after.

Through a weekend retreat, Deborah begins to grasp her calling: "I knew that I had a mission in life which had to do with

life — giving life and helping life in others." Thomas makes an Ignatian retreat and tells us that "knowing myself as a sinner who is loved to the death by Jesus Christ gave me a freedom to offer myself to be whatever the Lord wanted me to be." PAUL recounts the discernment that led to new service in the Church:

I had been asked to take a position in the diocese which would involve leaving my longtime work as an architect. My wife Elizabeth and I made a week-long Ignatian retreat together with the idea of discerning whether I should take the position in the diocese. During the retreat, it became very clear that I was supposed to do this. The clear understanding came during the retreat.

All the prayer was a confirmation. Elizabeth, too, through her prayer, was on the same page. We didn't make a full silent retreat, and we would speak together each evening about this. By the end of the retreat, it was very clear.

Discernment may be and at times must be done without such times of retreat. Nonetheless, those faced with important discernments may profitably consider how to find spaces of silence in their daily lives, and whether some form of retreat — a day, a weekend, or several days — might assist their discernment. When commitments do not permit time away, the Ignatian Exercises may also be made in daily life.[9] The experience of many confirms the value of such times of quiet and retreat for discernment.

Spiritual Direction

ERIC was in his mid-thirties, a highly successful business consultant. He shares his story:

I had thought about priesthood at times over the years but had never done anything about it. For fifteen years, since college, I always thought that I'd figure this out some day, but had never acted on it. I always went to Sunday Mass and never did anything really bad, but I was busy in the "forest" of the world. There were times when I would feel some heaviness inside, as though I was living too superficially — just living for passing things. On one business trip to Europe this really hit me, and I felt I had to do something about this. At the same time I knew that the woman I was dating wanted to know whether we were going to get married. I realized that I needed to make a choice.

All of this was working on me. Then, one Sunday, I went to Mass, and it was like God hit me over the head with a hammer. The Gospel was the call of the rich young man [Mark 10:17–22]. He asks Jesus, "Now what do I need to do?" And Jesus says, "Sell the things you have and follow me." It was like I was the only one in the church. It was like God saying: "I mean you, I'm talking to you." It was like a direct call to me. I was stunned.

At that point I knew I needed to act. I shared what had happened with the woman I was dating and my sense that I had to do something about this. Then I called the seminary. This was the point when I moved to action. The moment I made the call, things moved. After calling the seminary, I knew that I needed to speak with someone. I asked a priest at my parish and we began to meet. From that point on, a path opened up.

Everything changes for Eric, and a true process of discernment begins when he *speaks with spiritual guides:* "From that point on, a path opened up." The transition from ponderings in isolation to dialogue with a spiritual guide resolves the fifteen-year deadlock in Eric's discernment: "For fifteen years, since college, I always thought that I'd figure this out some day, but had never acted on it.... The moment I made the call, things moved."

Eric's experience highlights a key element in Ignatius's teaching on discernment. For Ignatius, discernment of God's will is always accompanied by a competent spiritual guide (*SpirEx*, 17). In fact, Ignatius wrote the book of the *Spiritual Exercises* as an aid to spiritual guides who assist others in discernment.

KAREN, too, discovers the value of such accompaniment. She says:

I had a good job, but I wasn't happy with the environment at work. I was also working with young adults at the parish, and that was fulfilling. I wasn't sure what God wanted. Should I continue in my job? Go on for my Ph.D.? Was it time to think more seriously about religious life? I just didn't know.

I had no spiritual director, so I phoned a priest I knew and we talked. He gave me the name of another priest who did spiritual direction, and I met with that priest. We've been meeting since then. It wasn't easy at first. I didn't know what spiritual direction was, and I wasn't yet ready to trust. But it has helped me a lot as I continue to discern. The director helped me to bring God into things, to become aware of God's presence throughout the day. I talk to God, and he talks to me; sometimes I don't listen. It took me awhile to see how God speaks, and I'm still learning a lot. I write things down so that I can look back over them.

Here too the transition from isolation to accompaniment in discernment opens a way beyond confusion, and sets in motion a process. Karen has not yet found her answer, but she is clearly on the way. Her account also reveals the spiritual learning that such accompaniment fosters: "The director helped me...to become aware of God's presence.... It took me awhile to see how.... I'm still learning a lot." Because she is wisely accompanied, Karen not only progresses toward discernment in a specific choice but also grows in spiritual formation.

In a different setting, **DENNIS** too is accompanied in discernment:

Carol and I had been married for two years. I was teaching in a college at the time and working toward my doctorate. In the parish I saw a deacon for the first time, a married man who was preaching and doing baptisms and weddings. I got very interested, and I told Carol that I'd like to do that. She said, "No, no way," because I was so busy with the teaching and the doctorate that she hadn't yet internalized my presence. There was an insecurity there, and so she wanted the deacon's role put on hold. What Carol was saying was that I couldn't be a deacon because I wasn't a husband yet. I couldn't give myself to others if I hadn't given myself to her. I was too busy with work and the degree.

I finished the degree and began teaching in another college. Three years later, we were walking home from Mass one Sunday when Carol said, "I think you should go be a deacon now." What she meant was that she had internalized my love, that we were in each other, that the discernment of the diaconate was built upon the protection of the marriage. I was sent out from the strength of that nuptial love into the sacrament of ordination as deacon. It was from the vocation of marriage; it was my spouse who sent me. She said, "You have to do this, this is who you are, this is what the Church needs." It was a deep discernment on her part. She said in effect, "Go, we are strong enough so that you can."

In the context of marriage, this narrative richly illustrates the difference between discernment in isolation and with appropriate sharing. Husband and wife *discern together,* and so with wisdom and fruitfulness.

When Anthony and Patricia discern their marriage, they speak with a sponsor-couple in Patricia's parish; they meet with the priest who would celebrate their wedding and, several times, with a priest they had known on retreat. Patricia adds: "Because we were both from divorced families, we consciously chose a solid married couple as our sponsors. I also spoke with one of my brothers who had a good marriage. I wanted wise counsel

from solidly married couples." When Michael is asked to take
a new position in a college, he speaks with his fellow priests,
seeks the help of his confessor, and asks the advice of close
friends.[10] With sure spiritual instinct, Anthony, Patricia, and
Michael seek to discern with the assistance of spiritually wise
persons.

There is obvious value in Ignatius's counsel that discernment
should be accompanied. When those who discern are unsure,
feel blocked, and do not know how to proceed, often the need
is for wise accompaniment. With such accompaniment, as Eric
says, a path opens before them.

Review of Spiritual Experience

KAREN says: "It took me awhile to see how God speaks, and
I'm still learning a lot. I *write things down* so that *I can look
back* over them." PATRICIA adds: "*I began journaling* the year
before I met Anthony, and did it daily with God during the
two years that led to our engagement. This also was a part
of my personal discernment process." Karen and Patricia both
practice another Ignatian principle in discernment: *conscious
review of spiritual experience* in order to grasp where God is
leading through it.

Ignatius invites those who discern not only to pray, but also to
review their experience of prayer (*SpirEx*, 77). He advises that
this be done immediately after the prayer when the experience
is still fresh and suggests that this may be done in writing.[11]
Because this conscious review leads to a deeper understanding
of God's workings in prayer, it solidly moves the discernment

process forward. Such review also provides valuable content for conversation with the one accompanying the discernment.

EDWARD shares his experience of this review:

> When I make the review, my attentiveness during the prayer is better. I started writing it to help me do it more faithfully. It makes the graces explicit. It's a confirmation of what happened in the prayer. I find that writing the review reinforces the habit of praying attentively.[12]

DENISE also comments:

> The key for me is writing things down. Then I can look back at what has happened in my prayer. It's about not forgetting. Then I can talk about it later in spiritual direction.[13]

Both Edward and Denise note that this review assists awareness of God's workings in prayer: "It makes the graces explicit." Both find that it aids attentiveness in prayer; both affirm the value of writing this review. Denise explicitly links the review of prayer with spiritual direction: "Then I can talk about it later in spiritual direction."

The God who is active in prayer is also active throughout the day. A further aid to discernment is the *examen prayer* (*SpirEx*, 43), through which the one discerning attends to God's workings beyond the formal time of prayer, in the course of the day. Ignatius's great esteem for this daily prayer as a means of discernment is widely recognized. Knowledge of and regular practice of the examen prayer will greatly bless the discernment process.[14]

From Preparation to Discernment

In Part One of this book:

We have discussed *preparation* for discernment.

We have clarified the *question* Ignatius poses for discernment: choices between good things by persons free to make such choices.

We have reviewed the *foundation* on which all discernment rests: awareness of an infinite Love that gives us life and purpose.

We have explored the *disposition* that alone permits discernment: a heart that seeks to respond to that love, and says, "Whatever you want, Lord."

Finally, we have discussed the spiritual *means* that Ignatius supplies toward growth in this disposition.[15]

This preparation for discernment is crucial. Without it, no true process of discernment is possible. By means of it, many problems in discernment are resolved. For these reasons, Ignatius dedicates a substantial part of the Spiritual Exercises to this preparation — a model for any process of discernment.

We are ready now to face a further question. It is the question I have heard more than any other in thirty years of working with discernment. Most probably, it is the question that led you to read this book. When you are discerning between good things that you are free to choose, and when you are striving to attain the disposition that permits discernment — when all of the preparation is substantially in place — *how will you know that you have found God's will?* How will you know that you have reached the clarity you seek?[16] How will the Robert of our first chapter, as he discerns between his love for Helen and his attraction for priesthood, *know that he has heard God's will rightly?* How will Monica *know that she has found God's will* in her decision between providing for her father at home or in a healthcare facility? How will Brian and Lisa *know that they truly have discerned God's will* in deciding whether Brian should begin medical school or not?

This question is crucial for those who love God: absence of an answer inhibits freedom for action; a clear answer brings peace of heart and releases energy for service.

In our spiritual tradition, Ignatius excels in the clarity of his response to this question. Through grace-guided reflection on spiritual experience, he identified three patterns in the way God replies to this question and formulated them succinctly in his Spiritual Exercises.[17] Those who learn these patterns — persons who discern and their spiritual guides — will find answers to this crucial question. They will find freedom to serve the Lord with new confidence and surety. Through Ignatius's teaching they will be equipped, in a new way, *to discern.*

In Part Two of this book we will explore that teaching.

PART TWO

DISCERNMENT

Chapter Five

Clarity beyond Doubting
The First Mode

Immediately, exulting in the Holy Spirit, he cried out: "This is what I want, this is what I seek, this is what I long to do with all my heart!" — Tommaso da Celano, *First Life of St. Francis of Assisi*

"He Could Not Doubt about the Matter"

In the first year of his conversion, Ignatius lived a rigorously penitential life. Among his practices was the resolve to abstain from meat. Ignatius later recounted the experience that changed this practice:

While he [Ignatius] was persevering in his abstinence from eating meat, and was so firm in this that he had no thought of changing, one day in the morning, when he had risen, some meat prepared for eating was represented to him, as though he saw it with his bodily eyes, without his having any desire for it beforehand. At the same time there came to him a great assent of the will that from then on he should eat it. And although he remembered his former intention, he could not doubt about the matter, but resolved that he

69

ought to eat meat. Relating this afterward to his confessor, the confessor told him that he should consider whether this might not be a temptation. But he, examining it well, could never doubt about this.[1]

In this experience, *something is shown to Ignatius:* that God does not want him to continue in a specific penitential practice. In the same moment, *Ignatius's will is strongly drawn* to what is shown him: "There came to him a great assent of the will that from then on he should eat it." And Ignatius simply *cannot doubt* that what is shown him is God's will: "And although he remembered his former intention, he could not doubt about the matter. . . . But he, examining it well, could never doubt about this."

Reflection on such experiences led Ignatius to identify a first "time" — that is, a first way, a first mode[2] — of how God reveals his will in choices between good options.[3] Ignatius describes this mode succinctly in the *Spiritual Exercises:*

> *The first time* is when God Our Lord so moves and attracts the will that, without doubting or being able to doubt, the devout soul follows what is shown to it, as St. Paul and St. Matthew did in following Christ our Lord. (*SpirEx*, 175)

In this brief text, Ignatius formulates a general teaching drawn from experiences like that described. Here we find again the same three elements:

something is shown to a person ("the devout soul follows *what is shown* to it"), the person's will is drawn to what is shown ("God Our Lord *so moves and attracts the will*"),

and the person cannot doubt that what is shown, and what so draws the will, is truly God's will (*"without doubting or being able to doubt"*).

Such experiences, Ignatius says, are a first way God may reveal his will to those who face choices between good options.[4]

Evidently, there is no extended process of discernment in this experience. Ignatius simply receives clarity as a gift from God. His part is to receive this gift and to act upon it. The same is true of all experiences of this mode of discernment: *if God chooses* to give this gift of clarity, our part is to accept and act upon it. If God does not choose to give this gift, then God is calling us to discern in other, more active, ways — the second and third modes of discernment, which Ignatius describes after this first.[5] We will explore these as well in subsequent chapters.

Some examples of this first mode of discernment will deepen our understanding, and help us to identify this mode in lived experience.

"This Certitude and Deep Peace"

MALIA'S experience of discernment is striking, and characterized by utter clarity.[6] The account follows:

A religious experience occurred in November of Malia's senior year of high school. Religious life as a lifestyle had never been a consideration for her. She remembers asking out of curiosity what kind of girl could become a nun. After naming some qualifications, sister turned to Malia and said, "someone like you. You could become a sister." Malia's response was a definite and silent, "no way!" Malia also recalls praying intensely to God and expressing her desire to do whatever he wanted her to do EXCEPT become a nun. These were the only times the subject ever came up and they were soon forgotten.

It happened on a Sunday morning, the last day of a weekend retreat made by the seniors. Malia had stopped to make a visit in the chapel. As she began to kneel down she experienced a powerful shock — like a lightning bolt that went straight through her from head to feet. She felt her whole being lifted up in a surging "yes!" She had no control over it. It was much like riding the crest of a wave — one must go with it. There were no images, no words, no arguments, no doubts, no reasoning process to make. It was decided — period! She knelt there a few seconds absorbing the impact. There was a sense of great peace and joy and direction. In fact, it was the only time she had ever experienced such certitude.

The decision was tested many times. In the course of the year the certitude never changed; neither did the deep inner peace and joy. . . .

It was this certitude and deep peace that carried her through the year, enabled her to leave home, and helped her weather the homesickness and discouragement of the novitiate. For years after, Malia would feel the powerful impact of the experience whenever she recalled it. It was a gift, and she confesses that she would never have made it [through those years] without it. It gave her a basic joyous outlook and confidence in life and the secure sense of being loved by God — a love that she could feel in a tangible way. In her late thirties Malia went through a period of spiritual desolation. Part of the desolation, the most painful part, was the loss of that sense of God's loving presence. And yet, in the midst of the confusion, guilt, and emptiness, the certitude of her vocation was left unshaken. It could not be doubted — when she had to believe that God was there, she knew he had chosen her to be his as a religious.

As she reflects on this, she believes that certitude comes from the fact that essentially the decision was God's; she only freely consented to accept it, to ride along on the crest of it.

Again we stand on holy ground. As she stops in the chapel, God simply showers grace upon Malia. She searches for images to express the abundance of the gift: a powerful shock, a lightning bolt, the crest of a wave.

In this experience, *something is shown* to Malia: the call to religious life and, with it, "also the name of the religious community." In the power of the experience, *Malia's will is attracted and moved* toward what is shown her: "She felt her whole being lifted up in a surging 'yes!'" And Malia *cannot doubt* that what is shown and what so attracts her is truly God's will: "There were...no arguments, no doubts, no reasoning process to make....It was the only time she had ever experienced such certitude....The certitude never changed....It could not be doubted." Clearly, Malia's vocational discernment occurs according to the first mode Ignatius outlines in his Spiritual Exercises.

As with Ignatius's experience, there is no extended process of discernment. Malia simply receives complete clarity as a gift from God; her part is to accept the gift and act upon it. This Malia freely does: "All that was needed was for Malia to follow through on the decision"; "She ... *freely consented* to accept it."

God's gift that Sunday morning sustains Malia throughout her entire religious life: "For years after, Malia would feel the powerful impact of the experience whenever she recalled it. . . . It gave her a basic joyous outlook and confidence in life and the secure sense of being loved by God." When desolation arises, this experience continues to support Malia.

"There Was No Doubting It"

ANDREW recounts a discernment made some years after his priestly ordination:

> I had been a diocesan priest for twelve years when I began to wonder whether God was calling me to be a Jesuit. I would receive images and suggestions in prayer which raised this question. As a diocesan priest, I had taught in college, been a university chaplain, and done spiritual direction. I wondered whether my background in education, spiritual direction, and retreat work was a sign that God was calling me to be a Jesuit.

When I was discerning my vocation as a priest, I had a clear sense of being drawn to parish work. I knew the Jesuits and had been in Jesuit schools. But I never thought of entering the Jesuits until one of them asked me if I'd ever thought of becoming a Jesuit. At that time, my attraction was to parish work. I delighted in that and found comfort in it. This attraction was confirmed in my seminary years, and I was confident about it. I made a thirty-day retreat before ordination as deacon, and the retreat confirmed my call to priesthood in the diocese.

Then, twelve years later, I began to feel a tug in prayer toward the Jesuits. The work I'd been doing seemed to fit, and there was an attraction to community life and vows. So there was something acting, something stirring there. I felt this desire. I raised it casually with my spiritual director; he noted it and said to just keep paying attention to it. It wasn't the centerpiece of my prayer. That focused on my relationship with the Father, Son, and Holy Spirit. But it would come back in discreet ways.

Things went on like this for some months. In the summer I made a retreat and there was curiosity, interest, and attraction there, but no light, no confirmation. I raised it again in spiritual direction, and the decision was not to take any active steps — not to speak with the bishop, for example. But the question was still there. During this whole time, while I was engaging this question, I continued my work as a diocesan priest.

Now the moment of clarity arrives in Andrew's discernment:

One day, my prayer had been a way of being with the Trinity. As the prayer was ending, almost as an aside, it was as though the Father were saying to me, "Oh, by the way, not as a Jesuit." Basically it was a clear no, a very clear sense of no. The Father had called me to be a diocesan priest. There was not a movement of the Holy Spirit toward religious life.

Almost immediately what came was the acknowledgment before the Father that I was in a kind of rut. In balancing all my work, there was a malaise. There were also tensions among some of the priests at that time. What came in the awareness of this rut, this dullness, was the invitation to be more serious about being a priest of my diocese. In bringing this to the Father, there was an immediate consolation and an invitation to the Father's own zeal, love, and care for the people I was serving, rather than just riding out the dullness with detachment. I found great freedom, great joy, and renewed delight in what I was part of in the diocese. The awareness that looking elsewhere, at religious life, was not of God and was distracting me from this subtle dullness, opened up the grace of new closeness to the Father in this.

This wasn't a startling experience. There had been a sense of intimacy with the Lord in the preceding prayer, and this was a conclusion to that. It was an invitation to more intimacy. There was perhaps something startling about it since I wasn't focused on this issue at that moment. There was a clarity, but also a consolation. God was showing me that he wanted to take care of me, showing me the rut and opening up the beauty of diocesan priesthood for me.

This came without seeking it in that prayer. It was just given, toward the end. It was clear. There was no doubting it. There was a great sense that this was not from me. I never explored the Jesuits anymore. I told my director about this, but it was the end. Once the rut behind it was exposed, it was the end. After that, I was able to live my diocesan priesthood with more life, closer to the other priests.

Andrew's experience also shows signs of Ignatius's first mode of discernment. *Something is shown* to Andrew: " 'Not as a Jesuit.' ... It was a clear sense of no, a very clear sense of no. The Father had called me to be a diocesan priest." *Andrew's will is moved and attracted* to what is shown: "I found great freedom, great joy, and renewed delight in what I was part of in the diocese." And Andrew *cannot doubt* that what is shown and what draws him is of God: "It was clear. There was no doubting it." Like Ignatius and Malia, Andrew simply receives the gift and acts accordingly: "I never explored the Jesuits anymore.... After that, I was able to live my diocesan priesthood with more life." Wisely, though he cannot doubt this clarity, Andrew shares his experience with his spiritual director.

MARGARET describes the moment when her own vocational discernment became clear:

Finally at the close of the semester, the answer came suddenly and stopped all questioning. "For you the ... cloistered life is the way to give Me everything. Others can do this in other ways, but this is to be your way." These may

not have been the exact words, but the message was unmis-
takable. There was never another question or doubt before
or after the Sisters accepted me into the . . . community.[7]

And THOMAS recounts his experience of prayer during an
Ignatian retreat:

In a moment of prayer, I experienced a flash of light in my
mind that I was truly called to be a Jesuit priest. That has
been the touchstone experience which has sustained my
vocation since my joining the Society of Jesus.[8]

Malia's experience of clarity appears to arise suddenly, outside
of any formal process of discernment. Her clarity is such that
no further process of discernment is necessary. As Andrew's
account indicates, and as is apparent in the full versions of Margaret's and Thomas's accounts, the moment of clarity beyond
doubting may arise within a process of discernment already
under way, and conclude it.[9] The first mode of discernment
may occur in either context. As the full versions also indicate, Margaret and Thomas, like Andrew, wisely speak of their
discernment with a spiritual guide.

"It Had Always Been Clear"

A final experience reveals yet another facet of this first mode of
discernment. GARY tells the story of his discernment:

I would find it hard to say exactly when my calling as a priest
first became clear to me. It was always there, in a sense.
It was there as far back as I can remember thinking about

my future, certainly already when I was in grade school. Faith was an important part of our family life, and we were always active in the parish. Catholic school also helped. So the spiritual soil for a vocation was there, though I was the only one of the three boys in the family that felt this call.

There was never any struggle about my vocation, never any searching to see whether God wanted me to be a priest. It was just clear to me and has always been clear to me since. I always had great esteem for marriage, and my parents were great examples, but I knew that it wasn't my call. I remember reading one of Thomas Merton's books once, and feeling all of this very strongly; I just longed to be a priest and live that life. It was all I wanted.

In my last year in college, when I had to decide what I would do, there was, in a sense, no decision to make: I knew that God wanted me to be a priest. I didn't know whether God wanted me to be a diocesan priest or a religious priest, and I spent that year looking into the diocese and several religious communities until I found my answer and entered the diocese.

I remember that when my ordination as deacon was about six months away, my spiritual director said that I needed to think well about it since this was the definitive commitment. I was willing to reflect but I knew, in my heart, that it was already clear. It had always been clear. It still is today, after thirty-seven years of priesthood.

For me, really, the only issue has always been fidelity to the calling, living it well, and never whether God called me

to priesthood or not. I've never doubted that and I can't
doubt it. I've always been grateful to God for that.

The dramatic experiences in the stories of Malia, Andrew,
Margaret, and Thomas are absent in Gary's account. The same
God-given clarity is there, however — a clarity that Gary simply
cannot doubt: "It was just clear to me and has always been clear
to me since.... I've never doubted that and I can't doubt it."
Stories like Gary's indicate that the first mode of discernment
may occur not only in dramatic but also in quiet, hidden ways,
yet with a deep certitude that the person cannot doubt — the
characteristic sign of the first mode of discernment.[10]
    We may note that while Malia's clarity concerns both her call
to religious life and the specific community to which God calls
her, the same is not true for Gary. Gary's clarity concerns his
call to priesthood: "I knew that God wanted me to be a priest."
Gary does not have this same first-mode clarity, however, with
regard to *where* God wills him to become a priest — whether
in his diocese or in a religious community, and, if this latter, in
which specific community. In this regard, Gary must continue
to discern. Such comparisons highlight the need to grasp clearly
"what is shown" in this first mode of discernment. We may also
note once again that Gary, like the others, notwithstanding his
sense of clarity, speaks with a spiritual guide.

First Mode of Discernment: Questions to Consider

Knowledge of this first mode alerts those who discern and their
guides to a first possibility in discerning God's will: that God

may simply grant the gift of clarity beyond doubting. The fruitfulness of such discernment is evident in the "certitude and deep peace," the joyous outlook, confidence, and "secure sense of being loved by God" that Malia experiences in her life; in the freedom, joy, and delight Andrew finds once more in his diocesan calling; in the complete freedom from doubt that Margaret and Thomas experience; and in the gratitude that Gary feels throughout his life.

As we have seen, discernment according to this first mode is God's freely bestowed gift. Our task, when God gives this gift, is to *recognize* the gift and to *act* upon it — as does each of the persons quoted in this chapter. To this end, those who discern and their guides will do well to reflect on the following questions.

What specifically was shown to the person? Was it, as with Malia, both a calling to religious life and to a precise religious community? Or, as with Gary, simply the calling to priesthood without further specification? In the experience, what *specifically* did God show the one discerning?

In the experience, *was there a clear attraction and drawing of the will* toward what was shown? Was there, as with Ignatius, "a great assent of the will"? As with Malia, "a surging 'yes!'"? As with Gary, a single-hearted drawing — "It was all I wanted"?

And *was it truly impossible for the person to doubt* that this discernment was of God? Like Ignatius, who "could never doubt" his discernment about a penitential practice? Like Malia, whose discernment "could not be doubted" through all the vicissitudes of life? Like Andrew, who says, "There was no doubting it"?

And *has the one discerning spoken with a spiritual guide* about the experience? For Ignatius, discernment, even according to this first mode, is never done in isolation.

Finally, *has the recipient of this gift acted upon it?*

There is an excellent reason that Ignatius mentions this mode of discernment first: when God gives this gift, no further discernment is necessary. Yet what should one do when God does not give this gift? Then, Ignatius says, God is calling us to discern according to a second or third mode. In our next chapter, we will explore the second of these.

Chapter Six

An Attraction of the Heart
The Second Mode

Walk till you hear
light told in music that was never heard,
and softness spoken that was not a word.
— Jessica Powers

"With Deep Devotion and Tears"

Ignatius is now fifty-two years old, the head of the Company of Jesus. He is discerning God's will regarding the poverty that he and his companions will live: Does God wish for them to live in radical poverty, with no fixed revenue at all? Or does God will some mitigation of this poverty for the good of the churches entrusted to their care? On Saturday, February 2, 1544, Ignatius begins a time of discernment. In his *Spiritual Diary*, he writes:

1. Saturday — Deep devotion at Mass, with tears and increased confidence in Our Lady, and more inclination to complete poverty then and throughout the day.

Ignatius describes similar experiences on the following days:

83

2. Sunday — The same, and more inclination to no revenue then, and throughout the day.

3. Monday — The same, and with other feelings, and more inclined to no revenue throughout the day....

4. Tuesday — An abundance of devotion before Mass, during it and after it, tears....I...felt more inclined to perfect poverty at the time and throughout the day....

5. Wednesday — Devotion before Mass and during it, not without tears, more inclined to perfect poverty....

6. Thursday — Before Mass with deep devotion and tears, and a notable warmth and devotion all through the day, being always moved more to perfect poverty.[1]

Here there is no single experience of absolute clarity as in Ignatius's earlier discernment regarding a penitential practice. Rather, day after day, a pattern repeats. In times of warm devotion, often accompanied by tears — that is, in times of *spiritual consolation* — Ignatius *consistently feels drawn to one option* in the discernment: that is, to complete poverty.

Later in the process, more troubling experiences enter. Ignatius writes:

When the Mass was finished and I was in my room afterward, I found myself utterly deserted and without any help, unable to feel the presence of my mediators[2] or of the Divine Persons, but feeling so remote and so separated from them as if I had never felt their presence and never would again.[3]

In this time of darkness, new thoughts arise:

Thoughts came to me at times against Jesus, at times against another Person, finding myself confused with various thoughts such as to leave the house and rent a room in order to get away from the noise, or to fast, or to begin the Masses all over again, or to move the altar to a higher floor in the house. I could find rest in nothing, desiring to end in a time of consolation and with my heart totally satisfied.

Ignatius now experiences the contrary of the earlier spiritual consolation. He feels spiritually deserted, without help, "remote and separated" from the Divine Persons — he experiences *spiritual desolation.* Troubling thoughts arise in the desolation, among them the thought of beginning the Masses over again, that is, of rejecting the entire process of discernment and beginning the discernment anew. In the darkness of *spiritual desolation,* the consistent inclination toward one option in *spiritual consolation* is attacked.

Unlike the discernment regarding the penitential practice, here a *process* of discernment unfolds over a number of days. We may also note Ignatius's profound, daily attentiveness to his interior experience. Each day he reviews the movements of his heart and their related thoughts; he then records these in writing for yet further reflection.

"Experience of Consolations and Desolations"

A second mode of discernment emerges from experiences such
as this. Ignatius formulates this mode succinctly in his *Spiritual
Exercises:*

> *The second time* is when sufficient clarity and under-
> standing is received through experience of consolations
> and desolations, and through experience of discernment
> of different spirits. (*SpirEx,* 176)

In this second mode of discernment, *discernment of spirits* and
discernment of God's will coincide: through discernment of
consolations and desolations — through discernment of spirits — a person attains "sufficient clarity and understanding" for
discernment of God's will — that is, sufficient clarity regarding
which option God wills in this choice.[4]

In a further document, Ignatius amplifies his description of
this second mode:

> Among the three modes of making a choice, if God does
> not move a person in the first mode, one should dwell
> persistently on the second, that of recognizing his voca-
> tion by the experience of consolations and desolations; in
> such manner that, as he continues with his meditations
> on Christ our Lord, he observes, when he finds himself in
> consolation, to which part God moves him, and likewise
> when he finds himself in desolation. And what consola-
> tion is should be well explained; that is, spiritual joy, love,
> hope in things of above, tears, and every interior movement
> which leaves the soul consoled in our Lord. The contrary

of this is desolation: sadness, lack of confidence, lack of love, dryness, etc.[5]

When, Ignatius says, God has not given the clarity beyond doubting of the first mode, the one discerning (and this person's spiritual guide) should turn to the second. The background to such discernment is ongoing prayer centered on Jesus in the Gospels: "as he continues with his meditations on Christ our Lord."[6] Like Ignatius in his *Spiritual Diary*, this person should attentively observe "when he finds himself in *consolation,* to which part [which option in the choice] God moves him, and likewise when he finds himself in *desolation."* Discernment according to the second mode presumes, then, that the one discerning understand and recognize experiences of spiritual consolation and desolation. Ignatius insists, therefore, that these "should be well explained" by the spiritual guide to the one discerning. In the Spiritual Exercises, Ignatius provides ample descriptions of both precisely for this purpose.[7] Because, finally, "as in *consolation* the *good spirit* guides and counsels us more, so in *desolation* the *bad spirit"* (*SpirEx,* 318), a clear mode of discernment now emerges.[8]

Those whom God has not called to discern according to the first mode, Ignatius says, are to turn to this second. They are to *pray regularly on the life of Jesus in the Gospels.* As they do so, they are to be attentive to their spiritual experience: to *review* this experience, and perhaps — like Ignatius — to record it in writing. Their spiritual guides are to explain well the nature of *spiritual consolation* and *spiritual desolation,* such that these persons will recognize these experiences when they occur. They are to discuss such experiences of spiritual consolation and spiritual desolation with their spiritual guides (*SpirEx,* 17), with whom they are to maintain regular contact throughout the discernment.

In their personal review and in conversation with their spiritual guides, they are to explore the following: In times of *spiritual consolation,* to which option have I felt inclined? Has this inclination *recurred? Enough* so that a clear pattern of inclination to one option when in spiritual consolation has emerged?[9] Enough so that, since "in consolation the *good spirit* guides and counsels us more," I may confidently judge, with the aid of my spiritual guide, that God is calling me to this option? Is this judgment further confirmed by the opposite inclination in time of *spiritual desolation* — the time when the *bad spirit* guides and counsels?[10]

Applied to Ignatius's experience in his *Spiritual Diary,* the consistent inclination toward complete poverty in time of spiritual consolation, and the attack on this inclination in time of spiritual desolation, strongly suggest that God wills Ignatius to choose complete poverty. In fact, after further discernment, Ignatius concludes that such is God's will.[11]

A look at further experiences will deepen our understanding of second-mode discernment, and help us to recognize it in practice.

"Again That Consolation Would Be Given Me"

RICHARD was discerning between marriage and Jesuit religious life. In January of that year, he decided that God was calling him to marriage; yet he was unable to find peace. He recounts the experience that resolved his struggle:

> The presence of sensible consolation when I reflected on joining the Jesuits was absolutely crucial for giving me the strength to make this decision. In retrospect it seems as though the Lord "tricked" me through this means to get past my own selfishness. Beginning in January of my senior year I began experiencing consolation during prayer in a way I never experienced before in my life. Indeed this was the beginning of my awakening to the Holy Spirit. I recall going up to church, sitting in front of the Sacred Heart altar, and being absolutely overwhelmed. This was the first time I had ever experienced this type of enjoyment from being with God. And this consolation was present whenever I reflected seriously on the possibility of entering the Jesuits. If I began to lose this desire, I would simply return to my parish church, sit in front of the Sacred Heart altar, and again that consolation would be given me. Throughout this period I knew instinctively that this was the right decision for me because of this consolation. I had not the slightest knowledge of a technical process for finding God's will by reflecting on my inner experience nor did I have the help of a counselor. I simply had a confirmation of sensible consolation. . . .

Richard applied to the Jesuits in March and, five months later, in August, entered the community. Of those five intervening months, he says:

I recall that I experienced many doubts in my own decision
to enter the Jesuits between the period of March to August.
But whenever I went to the church and sat in silence, my
experience of peace was restored and with it the conviction
that God was calling me.[12]

The crucial factor in Richard's discernment is "the presence
of *sensible consolation.*" Such consolation consistently accompanies one option in the discernment: "this consolation was
present *whenever I reflected seriously on the possibility of entering the Jesuits.*" And Richard knows that God's will is revealed
to him through this consistent pattern. When doubts occur, the
same consistent pattern confirms the discernment: "Whenever
I went to the church and sat in silence, my experience of peace
was restored and with it the conviction that God was calling
me." A recurring pattern of *spiritual consolation* ("my experience of peace") accompanied by *clarity regarding one option*
in the discernment ("and with it the conviction that God was
calling me") — this is the second mode of discernment. This
pattern repeats until Richard has received "sufficient clarity and
understanding," and his discernment concludes.

Richard's account indicates that, by contrast with the first
mode of discernment, *doubt* may enter second-mode discernment while the discernment is in process and before "sufficient
clarity and understanding" is received. It further reveals that
second-mode discernment is a *process* that unfolds gradually — in this case, over several months. As Ignatius says, the
heart of this process is spiritual *experience* — for Richard, the
experience of spiritual consolation.

"Only When There Was Peace in My Heart"

MARIA is discerning between active and contemplative religious life. She loves the active life of service, and yet is beginning to feel drawn to cloistered religious life. She shares her experience:

> This desire came as something of a surprise to me. Yet, it also gave me joy and peace. I prayed a lot about it because I wasn't sure if this were from God or me. One thing I did notice was that when troubles arose inside or outside of me, this desire was not strong. Only when there was peace in my heart did the desire come back and stay with me. This happened several times. I spoke with my confessor about it, and he encouraged me to follow whatever God was asking.[13]

Again *doubt* is part of the process. Again a *drawing in time of consolation* emerges: "Yet, it also gave me joy and peace. ... Only when there was peace in my heart did the desire come back and stay with me." Maria is aware of a *contrasting pattern* as well: "I did notice was that when troubles arose inside or outside of me, this desire was not strong." She is *attentive* to her spiritual experience: "One thing I did notice. . . . " And, wisely, Maria discusses this experience with her *spiritual guide*.[14]

Is this true second-mode discernment? Certainly, many elements of such discernment appear to be present. Yet Maria and her spiritual guide will need to explore several questions before this discernment may be decided. Are Maria's experiences of peace and joy and of interior trouble truly the *spiritual* consolation and *spiritual* desolation of which Ignatius speaks (*SpirEx*,

316, 317), and which alone permit second-mode discernment?[15] Is there a *sufficiently clear pattern* of drawing toward contemplative life in spiritual consolation? Of a contrasting inclination in time of spiritual desolation? Does Maria have the *"sufficient clarity and understanding* through experience of consolations and desolations" necessary for second-mode discernment? This does not appear to be the case. Most probably, this is a second-mode discernment that is still in process. Maria will need to continue the process through prayer, attentiveness to her spiritual experience, and conversation with her spiritual guide. Maria, as a prayerful and spiritually sensitive person, is an excellent candidate for such discernment. Clearly, Ignatius's teaching on second-mode discernment will greatly assist Maria and her guide as this process continues.

"The Room in My Heart"

In chapter 1, we listened as **ROBERT** shared the beginnings of his attraction toward priesthood:

> When I went to college I started going to daily Mass. That was where the idea of a vocation started to be stirred. I went to daily Mass all year. I was also making visits to the Blessed Sacrament. That was where I first felt deep, deep stirrings in my heart; I really started feeling the pull.

While at college Robert also began dating Helen and so entered the vocational struggle we have seen. Three years later, the moment of decision arrived:

I finished my degree and started teaching. Once I was talking with a friend who told me that I needed to do something, that I'd been on this marriage-priesthood seesaw for two or three years. I said to myself, "Yes, he's right. It's time for me to face this question."

Robert continues:

I said, "Okay, I'll go and give it a shot." I had the idea that it wouldn't work out and then I could go and marry without any problem.

The first semester was really hard, and when I went home for Christmas break I told my family I was leaving. I called the rector, and he said to spend a week with my family and talk about it. A priest I knew told me to spend a little time praying every day, asking that Christ would show me whether he was calling me to be a priest. I did, and Christ did show me: the call was to be a diocesan priest. It felt right. It was the same feeling I had before the Blessed Sacrament in college — that kind of certainty, that serenity that I wanted, and that attracted me to being a priest.

The seminary wasn't easy for me, and doubts would come back in different ways, mostly around celibacy. I talked about them with my faculty advisor and he helped me with them.

When I made a thirty-day retreat, it was the end of my lingering doubts. I dealt with all the struggles I had never really resolved about Helen. On that retreat, I went to the "room in my heart," that place that I had experienced in the chapel with the Blessed Sacrament in college, that intense serenity, this place where God lived. When I would go into that space in my heart, I would always experience that peace and serenity. Often I would not go there, but, when I did, there was this peace. I told the retreat director that I had not been in that room for a long time. I never missed the Liturgy of the Hours and the Rosary, but I had not gone into that room in my heart. On that retreat, I was entering that room, and I found my identity.

When I was ordained, at the laying on of hands, I had a profound, deep experience of absolute certitude that God wanted me to be a priest. It was like being back before the Blessed Sacrament — that serenity, that peace I want. I remember saying to myself, "Robert, if you ever doubt your vocation, remember this moment." I was never so certain of anything in my life before. It gave me great joy.

We stand on holy ground. Robert's discernment, with many struggles, over many years, is a *second-mode* discernment. In the midst of doubts and struggles, a pattern emerges: in time of *spiritual consolation,* Robert is drawn to *diocesan priesthood.* The experience before the Blessed Sacrament in college repeats throughout the entire process of discernment. Whenever Robert enters the "room in his heart," he experiences peace and serenity, with a drawing toward priesthood. Robert attains "sufficient clarity and understanding" through this repeated experience of spiritual consolation, and his discernment is clear: "I was never so certain of anything in my life before."

Robert's account also highlights the struggles which may be involved in attentiveness to spiritual experience: "I told the retreat director that I had not been in that room for a long time." Something in Robert resists entering the very interior space for which he so longs. He is not alone in such struggles. When Robert has the courage to stop, to open his heart to the Lord in prayer, and to notice what is stirring within, his discernment progresses surely.[16] We may also note the critical importance of spiritual accompaniment — his conversation with the retreat director — in gaining this courage.

"When I Was Most Joyful"

We have heard STEVEN and LAURA share their certitude that God willed their marriage.[17] Laura describes key moments in her personal discernment:

> Steven and I had known each other since the start of college. We had dated on and off for two years, and then seriously in our junior year. For me, the discernment happened long before then.
>
> In the middle of my sophomore year, during the January term, I did a service project. I spent three weeks teaching children in a grade school run by sisters. I loved being in the classroom with kindergarten and first-grade children as a teacher's assistant. Being with the children was a deeply joyful experience.
>
> I remember how beautifully contemplative the time was there. I would take bike rides, watch the birds out of my window, just slowing down. I remember being very peaceful. I don't remember thinking about Steven that

much. The time was quiet, peaceful, a joy; that's what I remember.

I was in the convent with the sisters. There was no huge moment of truth about religious life. I was just not drawn to it. That was a conscious discernment. The fact that I was living in a convent at the time that I was coming so alive with joy never said to me that I was being called to religious life. There wasn't any drawing to it. It never came up that the joy was due to a call to religious life. I never felt this.

The joy of being with the children built gradually. It was that intense joy that brought Steven to my heart, wanting to share that joy. One day I was sitting in the classroom with the children, feeling all of this. I thought, the only thing that could make this better would be if Steven walked through the door at this time and could share this with me. I loved the teaching. The one person I wanted to share it with was Steven. I knew that when I was most joyful, I wanted to share this with Steven.

I knew that the next step was marriage with Steven. In our junior year we began dating seriously, and, later that year, we got engaged.

This is a beautiful account of discernment by contrasting inclinations of the heart. In an unarticulated but clear way, Laura is conscious of *discerning God's will:* "That was a conscious discernment." In a setting conducive to choice for religious life — a peaceful place, the proximity of the sisters, a sharing in their teaching ministry, a growing joy — Laura clearly senses that she is not drawn to religious life: "It never came up that the joy was due to a call to religious life. I never felt this."

As Laura's joy in teaching intensifies, the clarity about her call to marriage with Steven grows. The awareness of calling crystallizes one day in the classroom: "I knew that when I was most joyful, I wanted to share this with Steven."

In an informal yet real way, the dynamic of second-mode discernment is at work here. A faith-filled woman, consciously seeking God's will, discerns between religious life and marriage and discerns God's call to marriage with a specific person, through awareness of the inclinations of her heart: "There was no huge moment of truth about religious life. I was just not drawn to it. That was a conscious discernment"; "I knew that when I was most joyful, I wanted to share this with Steven. I knew that the next step was marriage with Steven." Through the experience of dating in the following year, through personal and shared prayer, and through conversation with wise spiritual persons, Laura's discernment is confirmed.

Persons called to discern in this way may ask themselves: "Do I have the *disposition* Ignatius describes" — "Whatever you want, Lord"? Are you using the *spiritual means* to grow in that disposition? Do you, like Laura, seek *spaces of quiet* that assist discernment? Are you, like Laura, *attentive* to your spiritual experience? Are the inclinations and disinclinations of your heart truly inspired by God — truly *spiritual?*[18] Are you *speaking* of your discernment with a person of spiritual wisdom?

"Like a Magnet Drawing Me"

JESSICA tells of her discernment:

My life is like a symphony. (I'm an organist.) The opening
theme was when I was in high school, sixteen or seventeen years old. There was an elusive kind of feeling, like
a magnet drawing me. I loved being in church, the liturgy,
the music. It all drew me.

Before high school I had thought of religious life, but not
a lot. I just used to admire the sisters. But I didn't put too
much thought into it. I dated. I had a couple of boyfriends,
and I enjoyed life.

One day during religion class, when I was a senior in
high school, I looked out the window. I could see the cross
on the top of the steeple of the parish church. I was drawn
to that like a magnet drawing me.

I went to daily Mass. There was something about Mass
that drew me. I used to love to listen to the Scriptures.
"Being drawn like a magnet" was a happy experience.
There was a stillness about it. I used to like to look at the
cross, listen to the music in church, all of this.

During our conversation, I asked Jessica if she could describe
the happiness she felt in "being drawn like a magnet." She
answered:

I entered into it. It was so elusive. I would watch the censor,
the incense, the stain-glass windows. I was just so involved
in it. And I felt alone with it — I couldn't share it. I didn't

think anyone would understand this. It was just being in this kind of atmosphere, being still, and enjoying it.

Jessica continues:

> At times I would be at a dance and it would be fun, but I always felt that there was something more for me. And the "more" was God. As a junior in high school, I was seriously thinking about religious life. By the time I was a senior, I knew. There wasn't one moment. It was a process, over time.
>
> I'd be at a dance or at a symphony or other social events, and I'd know there was more for me. I'd be happy with people, with friends. I'd be joyful, having a good time, but I'd feel like there was more for me, more that was drawing me. The "more" was God calling me to be his bride. When I told my parents, they cried, and I said, I have to go. There was such a drawing, like a magnet draws.

Jessica thought of all she had shared, and concluded, "It's God's story with me. A love affair."

A repeated drawing, "like a magnet," accompanied by spiritual joy; a recurring sense that "there was more for me" even when enjoying a healthy social life; a search nourished by faithful, daily prayer; a "process, over time" of increasing attraction to one option; a point when sufficient clarity and understanding is reached regarding that option: this is discernment according to the second mode. As Jessica says so simply and so profoundly, her discernment is a love affair.

Second Mode of Discernment:
Questions to Consider

As we have seen, second-mode discernment is discernment of God's will through *discernment of spirits* — "through experience of consolations and desolations." Ignatius offers his Rules for the discernment of spirits (*SpirEx*, 313–36) precisely to assist in such discernment. If God calls us, like Richard, Maria, and others we have seen, to discern according to the second mode, then the greater our knowledge of these Rules, the better prepared we will be to discern. Growth in our capacity for second-mode discernment occurs through growth in understanding discernment of spirits. The means for such growth are many: Ignatian retreats with experienced directors, reading, classes, and, as we have said so often, accompaniment by spiritual guides knowledgeable in discernment.[19] As this learning grows, a delight also grows. With marvel, we discover that it truly is possible to hear the "still small voice" of God speaking in our hearts: the often confusing clash of attractions and resistances gives way to spiritual clarity.

As Ignatius indicates, second-mode discernment takes place through experiences of spiritual consolation and spiritual desolation. Such discernment requires that, like Richard, Maria, Laura, and the others, we *note* such experiences when they occur. Faithful attention to this experience allows us to grasp any emerging patterns of attraction and resistance. As Jessica says, second-mode discernment is not given in "one moment" but is "a process, over time."[20]

Above all, such discernment requires the *accompaniment of a spiritual guide:* to instruct us in discernment of spirits, to teach

us attentiveness to spiritual consolation and spiritual desolation, to guide our growing experience of discernment of spirits,
and to question opportunely or to confirm the emerging results
of the discernment. Such guidance assists in avoiding many pit-
falls and opens a sure path to second-mode discernment, when
God calls us to such discernment.[21]

Second-mode questions, then, concern whether God is giving
"sufficient clarity and understanding" through the "experience
of consolations and desolations," and through the "experience
of discernment of different spirits."[22] But what if, though they
do all that second-mode discernment requires, including being
attentive to experiences of spiritual consolation and spiritual
desolation, and speaking with a spiritual guide, those discerning
do not find "sufficient clarity and understanding" for discernment? What then for persons like Richard, who must discern
between marriage and Jesuit religious life, Maria, who must
discern between active and contemplative religious life, Laura,
who must discern a call to marriage with Steven, or those who
face any significant choice? Then, Ignatius says, God is calling
them to discern according to a third mode. We turn now to this
third way of discerning.

Chapter Seven

A Preponderance of Reasons
The Third Mode

Better than anyone else, the Holy Spirit will teach you how to taste with the heart and carry out with sweetness what reason shows to be for the greater service and glory of God.
— St. Ignatius of Loyola

A Further Mode of Discernment

In our preceding chapter, we accompanied Ignatius through several days of discernment regarding poverty. As we have seen, during those days Ignatius attentively notes experiences of spiritual consolation and spiritual desolation: he discerns according to the second mode. Simultaneously, however, Ignatius prayerfully reviews the *concrete factors* in this discernment: What advantages and what disadvantages for God's service will follow if he and his companions adopt a mitigated poverty? A more radical poverty? He further asks: Does the review of these advantages and disadvantages *reveal God's will* in this discernment? Clearly, Ignatius here adopts a further mode of discernment, no longer based on experience of consolation and desolation, but on consideration of the advantages and disadvantages for God's service related to either option.

Ignatius identifies various *advantages* to a *mitigated poverty*: the Society of Jesus will be better maintained; its members will not trouble others by begging; they will be less exposed to disordered concern for their material welfare; the time necessary for begging will be free for ministry; their churches will be better maintained and so foster greater devotion, and so forth. But Ignatius also perceives *disadvantages* to a *mitigated poverty*: the members will be less diligent in helping others, less ready to go on journeys and endure hardships, and less able to draw others to true poverty.

When Ignatius considers the *advantages* of *radical poverty*, the list grows long: the members will have greater spiritual strength through closer imitation of Jesus who lived in such poverty; they will overcome worldly avarice more easily; they will be more united through sharing the same complete poverty; they will more readily hope for everything from God; they will live more humbly and more united with their humble Lord; they will be less inclined to desire worldly consolation; they will give greater witness as others see that they do not desire worldly things, and so forth. The list extends to seventeen reasons.[1] Ignatius considers that the *disadvantages* of *radical poverty* coincide with the advantages of mitigated poverty already outlined, and does not repeat them.[2] Clearly, for Ignatius, a preponderance of reasons favors the choice for radical poverty.

As is evident, this mode of discernment reviews the *reasons* that support one or the other option and attempts to identify toward which option the greater weight of reasons inclines. As

Ignatius's list of reasons further reveals, these are *spiritual reasons* — reasons based on faith and on the greater service of God. In Ignatius's vocabulary, these are reasons that suggest that the option considered will be for *God's greater glory,* that is, that this option, more than the other, will serve to make God known and loved in human hearts.

When, Ignatius says, God has not shown his will by the first mode of discernment (clarity beyond doubting), and when sufficient clarity and understanding have not been given through the second (experience of consolations and desolations), we are to proceed to this third mode of discernment.[3] We turn now to his text in the Spiritual Exercises.

A Time of Tranquility

The third mode of discernment presumes a time when the one discerning is calm and tranquil and so can reflect well on the reasons for each alternative. Ignatius writes:

> *The third time* is one of tranquility, when one considers first for what purpose man is born, that is, to praise God our Lord and save his soul, and, desiring this, chooses as a means to this end some life or state within the bounds of the church, so that he may be helped in the service of his Lord and the salvation of his soul. I said a tranquil time, that is, when the soul is not agitated by different spirits, and uses its natural powers freely and tranquilly. (*SpirEx,* 177)

This is a heart neither powerfully stirred by spiritual consolation nor troubled by spiritual desolation — a heart that is "not

agitated by different spirits," and so "uses its natural powers
freely and tranquilly."[4] A heart in such *a tranquil time,* Ignatius
says, may approach third-mode discernment.

A companion describes Ignatius's practice of discernment
according to this third mode:

> When he wrote the Constitutions and when he decided
> something of great weight and importance, as we said, he
> always first consulted with the Lord about it in prayer; and
> the way he did this was the following. First he emptied
> himself of any passion or attachment which often confuse
> and obscure judgment so that it cannot discover as easily
> the radiance and light of the truth, and he placed himself,
> without any fixed inclination or predetermined direction,
> like matter ready to take any shape, in the hands of God
> our Lord. After this, with great energy he asked of God
> grace to know and to embrace the better choice. Then he
> considered with great attentiveness and weighed the rea-
> sons which presented themselves for one option and for
> the other, and the strength of each, and he compared them
> among themselves. Finally, he turned again to our Lord
> with what he had thought and what he had found, and
> reverently placed it all before his divine gaze, beseeching
> him that he would give him light to choose what would be
> most pleasing to him.[5]

Before he discerns, Ignatius seeks freedom from "any passion
or attachment" which might obscure or confuse his judgment.
He enters third-mode discernment only when able to use his

natural powers freely and tranquilly. Such is the condition of heart necessary for the third mode of discernment.

If the heart is *not* calm — is not in "a tranquil time" — the third mode of discernment should not be attempted. In this event, those discerning must first seek peace of heart; once this is present, third-mode discernment may be attempted.

We begin the third mode, Ignatius says, with a *consideration* and a *desire* (*SpirEx,* 177). Those discerning consciously *consider* the foundation on which all discernment is built: the Love that has given them being and purpose, and that calls them "to praise God our Lord" with their lives and so rejoice in eternal communion with God. Through this consideration they clearly perceive, as they begin, that all true discernment is the choice of "a *means* to *this end.*" And, Ignatius says, if they would discern well, their deepest *desire* must be to attain this end.

Third Mode of Discernment: First Way

Ignatius now offers practical ways of discerning according to the third mode.[6] The first of these, Ignatius writes, contains six points.

First Point: The Question

The first point, Ignatius says, is "to place before myself the thing about which I wish to make a choice" (*SpirEx,* 178). For Ignatius, in the example cited above, this is the choice between mitigated and radical poverty. For Monica, this is the choice between caring for her father at home or with the help of a nursing facility. For Brian, this is the choice between his present work and pursuing medical studies. The first step in the discernment is to see the question clearly.

Second Point: The Disposition

As we have seen, this is the heart that says, "Whatever you want, Lord." You approach the discernment, Ignatius says,

> *without any disordered attachment,* so that I am not more inclined or disposed to accept the thing before me than to refuse it, nor to refuse it rather than accept it, but that I find myself *like a balance at equilibrium,* ready to follow whatever I perceive to be *more for the glory and praise of God our Lord* and *the salvation of my soul. (SpirEx,* 179)

Such is Ignatius's own practice in third-mode discernment:

> First he emptied himself of any passion or attachment which often confuses and obscures judgment so that it cannot discover as easily the radiance and light of the truth, and he placed himself, *without any fixed inclination or pre-determined direction,* like *matter ready to take any shape,* in the hands of God our Lord.

This disposition alone permits third-mode discernment. Those who would discern in this way must determine: Do you have this freedom? Are you like "a balance at equilibrium" between the two options, ready to choose whatever you perceive to be "more for the glory and praise of God our Lord and the salvation of your soul"?

Third Point: The Petition

The next step, Ignatius says, is *"to ask God our Lord* that he be pleased to move my will and place in my soul what I ought to do in the matter before me that would be more for his praise and glory" (*SpirEx*, 180). Before discerning, you humbly and trustingly ask for the gift of *a mind that will see clearly,* and *a will that will choose faithfully* what is more for God's praise and glory — what will make God more known and loved in human hearts, in this life and the next. His biographer writes that when Ignatius was ready to discern, "with great energy he asked of God grace to know and to embrace the better choice."

Fourth Point: The Reasons

Now, Ignatius says, you are ready to consider the advantages and disadvantages of either option. As noted, these are *spiritual and faith-based* advantages and disadvantages, "solely for the praise of God our Lord and the salvation of my soul" (*SpirEx*, 181).[7] His biographer describes Ignatius's practice of this fourth point: "Then he *considered with great attentiveness* and *weighed the reasons* which presented themselves *for one option and for the other,* and the *strength of each,* and *he compared them among themselves.*"

Ignatius's practice and the experience of many suggest the value of doing this in writing: of outlining in writing, under both options, the advantages and disadvantages you see for God's greater glory in the choice you face.[8] As you write, and as you review what you have written, you are likely to perceive more clearly where the preponderance of reasons lies.

Such writing also facilitates sharing with the spiritual guide who accompanies the discernment.

Fifth Point: The Choice

As Ignatius reflects on the advantages and disadvantages of either option, a moment comes when he judges that the preponderance of reasons lies with radical poverty:

> In the afternoon, for an hour and a half or more, I once more went through the choices, and made the choice for complete poverty. I found myself with much devotion, with a certain elevation of soul, and with great tranquility, without any opposing desire to possess anything. I lost the desire of proceeding further with the process of choosing as I had thought of doing some days earlier.[9]

Though both options will promote God's glory, Ignatius now perceives that radical poverty presents a preponderance of reasons for God's glory — more than mitigated poverty, it will serve to make God known and loved. In the fifth step of third-mode discernment, Ignatius says, "after I have *thought and reasoned* in this way *about every aspect* of the matter before me, I will look to see *toward which alternative reason inclines more*" (*SpirEx*, 182).[10]

Sixth Point: The Confirmation

Once Ignatius has chosen, he adds a further step to his discernment. His biographer continues: "Finally, he turned again to our Lord with what he had thought and what he had found, and reverently placed it all before his divine gaze, beseeching him that he would give him light to choose what would be most pleasing to him." Before he concludes his discernment, Ignatius brings it to God and asks that God *confirm* his choice.

Ignatius writes: "Having made this choice . . . the person who has made it should, with much diligence, turn to prayer before God our Lord and offer him this choice, so that his Divine Majesty may be pleased to receive and confirm it, if it is to his greater service and praise" (*SpirEx*, 183). In the great devotion, the elevation of soul, the great tranquility, the absence of any opposing desire, and the sense of completion in the process which follow upon Ignatius's choice of radical poverty, we find a first indication of how God may give such confirmation. We will return to this point in the next chapter.

"She Suggested Looking at the Advantages and Disadvantages"

An example will illustrate this third mode in daily life. PATRICK shares his story:

> When I was downsized by my company, I began my own business. Around the same time I had begun to get involved as a volunteer in prison ministry, and this ministry was very rewarding. After a time, the person who ran prison ministry for the diocese had to move, and I was offered the position. It was a full-time position. I said no. I didn't want a full-time job with prison ministry. I just wanted to stay as a volunteer.

A few days passed and I was unsettled, not sure about this, still fighting the new position. I told my wife, Donna, about it. I told her that I'd been praying, but that I wasn't sure how to discern. Donna was taking courses, preparing to be a spiritual director, and had almost completed the program. She offered to help. I knew she could help me, and that's why I asked her about this.[11]

Now Patrick begins an active process of discernment:

Donna suggested that I spend an hour a day in prayer and gave me Scriptures for the prayer. So each day I went to the adoration chapel in the parish and prayed with a Scripture. But I didn't get any clarity yet.

Then she suggested looking at the advantages and disadvantages of taking the position and of not taking it. I did that. First I looked at the advantages of taking the position. There were a number of them. I knew the ministry well from my experience. I had the administrative skills from my career. I had a good background in theology, and that would help in directing the ministry in the diocese. I also knew that, if I took the position, I would be giving more of myself to the Lord. The disadvantages were that I would lose time for myself, time for the gym, for my grandkids, really, time to be lazy and not have to push myself. When I thought about not taking the position, all of this reversed.

I went through this exercise, but also continued with the Blessed Sacrament and Scripture. The whole process took about three weeks. That didn't matter to me; I wanted to do it well. About a week and a half into it, I found that all the selfish motives for not taking the position were gone. And it seemed like the reasons for taking the position were more solid.

Then Donna gave me the passage about Bartimaeus [Mark 10:46–52]. It was a passage I knew well, and I was sitting there reading it. When Jesus asked Bartimaeus, "What do you want me to do for you?" he answered, "I want to see." That's what I wanted, too. Then the last five words of the passage really hit me: Bartimaeus "followed him on the way." I felt something of what Bartimaeus must have felt because I too had started to lose sight in one eye a few years before, and the eye healed. It seemed to me that the Lord was asking me to follow him too, through the prison ministry. It hit me like a ton of bricks. It was amazingly clear what the Lord wanted. I spent three more days with this Scripture, seeking confirmation.

I've been doing the prison ministry for four years now, and I'm still sure that the discernment was clear.

With Donna's help, Patrick begins his discernment according to the second mode. When he does not find "sufficient clarity and understanding" through "experience of consolation and desolation," Donna, following Ignatius's counsel, suggests that he try the third mode. As Patrick does so, he grows in the disposition necessary for discernment: "About a week and a half into it, I found that all the selfish motives for not taking the position were gone." He also realizes that the preponderance of reasons points toward taking the position. Finally, when Patrick prays about the healing of Bartimaeus, he is confirmed in this choice:

"It hit me like a ton of bricks. It was amazingly clear what the Lord wanted."

Third Mode of Discernment: Second Way

The second way is to be used, as necessary, after the first has been attempted.[12] If the review of advantages and disadvantages has not brought clarity, this second way may help to *reach such clarity*. If the review of advantages and disadvantages has brought clarity, the second way may serve to *strengthen that clarity*.[13] It contains, Ignatius says, four rules and a note.[14]

First Rule: The Disposition

Here Ignatius reaffirms the basic disposition that permits discernment: "that *the love which moves me and causes me to choose this thing* must descend from above, from the love of God; so that the one who chooses *should first of all feel in himself* that the love, greater or lesser, that he has for the thing he chooses, *is solely for the sake of his Creator and Lord*" (*SpirEx*, 184). The three rules that follow (*SpirEx*, 185–87) are ways of testing whether this is in fact my disposition, and, if necessary, of growing in it. Do I *sense this love in myself*, guiding my discernment? Do I, like Catherine as she drives home from work, grasp the depth with which I am loved, and seek to choose *solely* out of love for the One who loves me so deeply?

Second Rule: A Person I Have Never Seen

A first test follows. I consider a person I have never seen or known, and who faces the same choice I face. I desire all spiritual growth for this person. Which option would I counsel this person to choose? Then, Ignatius says, I will follow the counsel that I give to the other (*SpirEx*, 185).

Would Brian counsel another man whom he does not know, and for whom he desires all spiritual growth, to continue in his present work or to begin medical school? Would Monica counsel another woman whom she does not know, and for whom she desires all spiritual growth, to care for her father at home or through a nursing facility?

This simple yet powerful exercise, in allowing me to view my choice from a distance — as another person's choice — helps me to gain an objective view of the choice itself, and so to choose with greater freedom.

Third Rule: When Life Is Ending

Ignatius offers a second test. I consider myself at the point of death, when all lesser motivations will lose their force, and all that will truly matter to me is to have loved God and fulfilled God's will. At that time, and viewed with that clarity, what choice will I wish to have made in my present discernment? Guided by this clarity, Ignatius says, I will make that same choice now (*SpirEx*, 186).

This second test, like the first, assists the one discerning to choose objectively, and so with freedom.

Fourth Rule: In the Light of Eternity

Ignatius proposes one final test. I see myself on the day of judgment and consider how, at that time, I will wish to have chosen in the present discernment. Then, Ignatius writes, I will make that same choice now (*SpirEx*, 187).

We may note that the judgment here is not between eternal loss and eternal life. The person is not choosing between good and evil, but between two goods, one of which promotes God's greater glory. The judgment will concern whether, in this choice, I have loved fully the One who loves me infinitely, or whether I have loved with reservation. The desire to have loved fully I will feel then, Ignatius says, will assist me to choose now with unreserved love.[15]

Once again, a simple but powerful exercise helps the one discerning to gain objectivity, and so greater freedom in choosing as God desires.[16]

A Note: The Confirmation

Once the choice has been made, the one discerning is to seek God's confirmation of this choice (*SpirEx*, 188). Everything said about such confirmation in the first way of third-mode discernment applies in this second way as well: "Having made this choice...the person who has made it should, with much diligence, turn to prayer before God our Lord and offer him this choice, so that his Divine Majesty may be pleased to receive and confirm it, if it is to his greater service and praise" (*SpirEx*, 183).

"When I Took the First Point"

An example here will illustrate how the second way may strengthen the first. RAYMOND shares his experience:

I had been pastor in my parish for thirteen years. The work was going well and I was grateful, but I was becoming physically and emotionally worn out. It was a big parish, with a school, and things had not been in good shape when I first came to the parish. Over the years we had turned things around, but it had taken a toll on me. I remember one evening when I first began to wonder whether I could continue as pastor, or whether I might need a change.

I talked about it with my spiritual director, and he encouraged me to let the bishop know my situation. A few weeks later I did speak with the bishop, and it was a good conversation. He knew about my situation. He told me that he was happy with my work in the parish and that if I wanted to continue, that would be fine. But he also said that he saw my tiredness, and that he wanted me to discern what I thought I should do. He would honor whatever decision I would make.

The bishop's response was encouraging, and I was willing to discern. Still, to discern about a position I'd had for so long was not easy for me. When I met with my spiritual director, he told me not to try to discern right away — that the issue was to become free enough to choose well. So I continued to pray, and we continued to meet. About five weeks later, when we met, he thought I was free enough then to discern whether I should stay at the parish or ask for another assignment. He suggested that I continue to pray, and that I try St. Ignatius's third time of election [third mode of discernment].

Now the active process of discernment begins:

> A week later I did try it. I sat in the rectory chapel with a
> notebook, and wrote down the advantages I could see in
> staying on as pastor, and the disadvantages. I did the same
> thing with the possibility of taking another assignment from
> the bishop. When I considered everything — the fact that
> I had been pastor for thirteen years and had given pretty
> much what I could; the effort it was costing me now just to
> do the daily work of pastor there; the real danger that, if I
> tried to continue, I was likely to get dangerously exhausted
> and have to stop anyway; the fact that things were in good
> shape and that there were others who could step in; my
> sense that I could do more good by a change that would
> help me start again with new energy rather than dragging
> in my work the way I was doing — it seemed to me that the
> greater good was to have someone else take over and that
> I get a fresh start in another assignment. As far as I could
> see, following St. Ignatius, this was saying that God's will
> was that I should ask the bishop for another assignment.
> But I still wasn't sure, and I wasn't ready to act.
>
> I shared all this with my spiritual director, and he sug-
> gested that I now try the second way St. Ignatius gives.
> About three days later, I did that in the same chapel. When
> I took the first point — where you think of another person
> facing the same decision and what you would say to that
> person — it really hit me. I knew immediately that I would
> never ask another person to continue in the same ministry
> with such deep exhaustion. I don't think I ever went past

this first consideration in the second way. This was so clear that I felt I had my answer.

When I shared this a few days later with my spiritual director, he agreed that this seemed very clear. He thought the discernment process was now concluded, that there was nothing more that needed to be done, and that it was time to speak with the bishop.

A few days later I did. The bishop agreed with the discernment and thought that the reasons sounded right. It was the final piece in the discernment. Within a few days I started to feel real happiness, a deep peace about the discernment, a certainty that I was doing God's will. This was the point I had always wanted to reach in the whole process.

In Raymond's story, the wisdom of Ignatius's two ways in the third mode of discernment is apparent. The second way, used after the first, removes any remaining doubt. The two ways together lead to a clear discernment, the tentative result of the first strengthened by the second: "This was so clear that I felt I had my answer."

Third Mode of Discernment: Questions to Consider

Those discerning and their spiritual guides may find the following questions helpful when they undertake third-mode discernment:

Before you begin this discernment, have you researched well the options in this choice? Do you *know the relevant data,* so that your consideration of advantages and disadvantages will be solidly rooted in the real situation?

As you begin this discernment, are you truly in *a tranquil time?* Able to use your "natural powers" freely and tranquilly?

As you begin, have you renewed your awareness of and desire for the *end* to which this choice is a *means:* to respond with love to God's infinite love for you, to promote God's greater glory in human hearts, and to progress toward the joy of eternal communion with God?

Are you spiritually *free,* open to either option, like a balance at equilibrium, ready to choose whatever you will perceive to be for God's greater glory?

Have you *sought God's help* in prayer before you consider the advantages and disadvantages of either option? Have you carefully considered these? Listed them in writing? Are these *faith-based* reasons, that is, advantages or disadvantages from the perspective of *God's greater glory?*

Do you see *which option* is favored by a preponderance of reasons? Do you see this clearly? If not, have you used the *second way* of the third mode?

Have you shared this process with a *spiritual guide?*

When you have chosen one option, have you brought this choice to God for *confirmation?* Have you received such confirmation?[17]

Ignatius's teaching on third-mode discernment highlights God's desire that we engage our natural, human capabilities in discernment. That teaching offers us a wise and efficacious manner of proceeding as we employ these God-given abilities.

PART THREE

FRUIT

Chapter Eight

The Value of the Process of Discernment

This is the mystery of my life. Do not seek other explanations. I have always repeated the words of St. Gregory Nazianzen: "In your will is our peace."
— Blessed John XXIII

Concluding the Process

When Ignatius reviews the reasons for mitigated and radical poverty and understands that God calls him to choose radical poverty, his heart is filled with peace. As we have seen, he writes: "I found myself with much devotion, with a certain elevation of soul, and with great tranquility, without any opposing desire to possess anything." At the same time, he senses that the process is complete: "I lost the desire of proceeding further with the process of choosing as I had thought of doing some days earlier."[1] Ignatius senses that no further discernment is necessary because the conclusion is already clear. Here Ignatius receives confirmation of his choice through *spiritual consolation* and a *sense of completion* in the process.

As Ignatius continues to pray, further experiences deepen this sense of confirmation: *additional reasons* for choosing radical

123

poverty, *greater strength in those already seen, increased move-*
ment of will toward this choice, and the sense that he has *done*
all he can, and *has found God's will.*[2]

When Patrick concludes his discernment regarding prison
ministry, he notes: "It was amazingly clear what the Lord
wanted. I spent three more days with this Scripture [Barti-
maeus], seeking confirmation." And when Raymond concludes
his discernment about his role as pastor, he says: "Within a few
days I started to feel *real happiness,* a *deep peace* about the
discernment, a *certainty that I was doing God's will.*"

DONALD'S discernment concludes in a similar fashion:

When I had tried the seminary a few years earlier, every
day I had the question: Do I belong here? I had no sense
that I could live the fullness of that vocation in joy. There
was always a restlessness. It was very hard for me when I
realized that this was not my call, since I desired so badly
to be a priest. It was only later that I would see the difference between my own idea that I should be a priest and a
vocation as a call from God.

When I met Angela, there was no turbulence. Now the
vocation was *given* to me in her particularity. I was free. My
vocation had found me; Angela had found me. I saw her
and I said, there's my wife. This time there was a sense of
being found. The search was over, the restlessness was over.
I consciously thought, "I have found God's will." There was
a sense that we could live the problems of this vocation in
joy. Here, the fullness of vocation was offered to me, as a
husband and a father, and I could live it in joy.

As we listen to Donald, we sense that *the process is complete:* "The search was over. ... I consciously thought, 'I have found God's will.' " The lifting of long-experienced restlessness, the sense of joy and fullness, and, consequently, his clear perception of God's call to marriage with Angela, tell Donald that the discernment is concluded.

MARIA reflects on the years of discernment that led her to her religious community:

> How did I know that this was where God was calling me? I was not looking for the perfect community; I was looking for God, for his Will for me. I realize now that this "understanding" was his gift and with it came another gift — that peace which surpasses understanding that only the Holy Spirit can give. These were not things I could give myself.[3]

Faithfully, and with guidance, Maria has discerned for several years. Now, the "peace which surpasses understanding that only the Holy Spirit can give" confirms her discernment. Maria knows that such understanding and such consolation are God's gift: "These were not things I could give myself." This abiding experience confirms her choice and tells her that her discernment is concluded.

ALBERT reviews the discernment that led him to priesthood:

> I have never forgotten my process of discernment and the many graces I received. It was truly a blessed time. It took years of youth retreats and mingling with young and old priests and religious to discover that God wanted me to

follow him in this unique way. But when I discovered my
vocation, I felt a great sense of peace and satisfaction that
served as a supernatural confirmation of my call. I was
certain this is what God wanted from me.[4]

Albert, too, experiences God's confirmation of his discernment:
"I felt a *great sense of peace* and satisfaction.... *I was certain*
this is what God wanted from me."

Experiences of this nature suggest that a personal process
of discernment is concluded. In some cases, like that of Raymond and his bishop, another will make the final decision. But
Raymond, like these others, has concluded his *personal* discernment. Wisely, he shares his conclusion with a spiritual guide.
Having done so, he is ready to act.

The Process and Growth

In this book we have listened as many have shared experiences
of discernment. For some, the process involved times of pain,
frustration, hesitation, and confusion. Why does a God who
loves us call upon us to discern? Why must Robert discern
between marriage and priesthood? Michelle between religious
life and marriage? Brian and Lisa between Brian's present job
and medical school? Monica between care for her father at
home or in nursing facility?

Certainly, *learning about discernment* — the purpose of this
book — will assist us greatly in the process of discernment.
Nonetheless, the question remains: Why does God call upon
us to discern? Why is a teaching like that of Ignatius necessary?

What role does the *process of discernment itself* have in God's loving providence in our lives?

In our search for an answer, we turn once more to an experience. REBECCA shares her story:

We were not a very religious family. We lived far from church, and it was not the most important thing in our lives.

When I was eighteen, I left home. I decided not to go to church unless I felt the interest. I felt that life was a big happy party. I got a job in a hospital and liked the work and where I was living. For a few years, I did a lot of partying.

One Saturday evening I went out for a party and didn't get back until early Sunday morning. There was a Catholic church nearby, and, as I was going to bed, the church bells rang. When I heard them, something stirred in me, and I said to myself, if I can be out all night for a party, I can go to Mass. I knew this was a God-moment, an eye-opening moment. I knew God was there. There was a deep feeling that something had to change. I realized that I did want God back in my life. At that point, I didn't know how to pray.

I got up and went to Mass. Nothing dramatic happened at the Mass, but I got to thinking, "What am I doing with my life?" I was twenty-three at the time. So I started going to Mass and helping in the parish. The hospital where I worked was run by sisters, and I started seeing them in a new way. I began talking to them.

I started teaching religion classes for kids, and I went to some parish missions. At the hospital, on lunch break, I would go to the chapel and would say to God, "What are you asking?" Things slowly started to come together. If someone had said the word "discernment" to me then, I wouldn't have had a clue what they were talking about.

I became interested in the sisters. There were four or five of them, and it was like I'd never seen them before. I was close to two or three of them and would have coffee with them, but we just talked in general and not about religious life.

Now Rebecca begins a more formal process of discernment:

The sisters invited me to a weekend retreat at their house. I had expressed some interest, nothing really definite. So I went, together with some other young women. As I drove in, I felt like everything was lifted from me, and I had an overwhelming sense of peace, like a homecoming. It felt just right. I didn't know what that all meant. That was when I really started asking questions.

After that weekend, I spent more time with one of the sisters at the hospital, and we started discerning together. She taught me to pray. I had a house, a car, and other things, and wondered whether I should dispose of them if I was going to enter. We worked together on this. I was also going with a young man and told him that we couldn't continue until I searched this out. Paul and I both thought that marriage would be the next step, but something was holding me back.

This went on for a year after that weekend. During this time, it felt right; I had that sense of peace and being home. I think I knew long before I told the sisters that I wanted to try it. I held back because of comments by others and because of Paul.

The peace was constant in those months. Only when others would strongly say I shouldn't do it would I waver. People saw that I loved to party and have a good time, and they didn't think I could make it in religious life. One who had been in religious life said it so strongly that it upset me. I quickly talked with someone and found peace again. Paul knew I was leaning this way and didn't try to stand in the way.

The decision just evolved. There really wasn't one moment that stands out. One day I was talking with the sister about disposing of my things, and she asked, "Would you like to enter?" I answered, "Yes." Then we started to put things in motion.

There have been hard times over the years, but I have always had that basic sense that it was right, that this is what I want, that this was really at the core. This core feeling has always been there.

Why does God ask Rebecca to discern? To discern about religious life? About her relationship with Paul? To spend three years in discernment? To experience, in the process, spiritual movements she does not understand? To face obstacles along the way? To reach clarity only gradually?

If we compare the Rebecca of the beginning of this discernment with the Rebecca of three years later when her discernment concludes, the enormous *human and spiritual growth* given through the process is evident.[5] Three years later,

Rebecca is no longer the young woman who feels that life is "a big happy party" and lives accordingly, with no concern for God and the life of faith. In those three years of discernment, Rebecca returns to the sacraments, learns how to pray, begins serving others in the parish, experiences spiritual direction, faces spiritual obstacles and overcomes them, and begins, without the vocabulary, to understand discernment of spirits: the meaning of a consistent attraction in time of spiritual consolation.

Certainly, discernment *is* about attaining clarity in a specific choice. We undertake discernment precisely because we seek such clarity. God, however, in calling us to the sometimes lengthy and laborious process of discernment, through it offers us a priceless and often life-changing *opportunity for growth*.

Through his troubled years of discernment, Robert gradually gains courage to enter that "room in his heart" where he encounters God's love and finds joy in his priesthood. Through many struggles in discernment, Michelle learns to surrender to God, discovers with immense joy God's great love for her, and, with new freedom, opens her heart to Scott's love and marriage. Through his discernment, Christopher learns that God is not "demanding and jealous," not a military commander, and adds, "The more I prayed, the happier I became." Through her process of discernment, Karen speaks to a spiritual director for the first time, learns to trust that accompaniment, grows in awareness of God's presence throughout the day, and observes, "I'm still learning a lot."

The examples of growth through discernment could be multiplied endlessly. It would be instructive to review *every story* in this book with this question in mind: What growth did God offer this person through the process of discernment? Our efforts and struggles in discernment have meaning in God's providence. Through them, the God who loves us calls us to new life and growth. The Ignatian teaching we have seen in this book is simply a guide to help us walk more surely, more resolutely, and more fruitfully along this path.

The Process and Grace

JAMES recalls the discernment that led to his religious and priestly vocation, and says, "It was a long process, not without its doubts and confusions and frustrations and dead ends." He continues:

> It was certainly the best decision I've ever made, and, amazingly, it seemed that God had made the decision for me. I hadn't sought an answer to the problem at all. The Great Problem Solver, as it turned out, had been at work on a problem that I had only dimly comprehended.[6]

"It was a long process, not without its doubts ... confusions ... frustrations ... dead ends": *human effort* in discernment is eloquently expressed here. "Amazingly, it seemed that God had made the discernment for me.... The Great Problem Solver ... had been at work": the wonder of *God's grace* at work in our discernment is compellingly expressed as well — "it seemed *that God made the discernment for me.*" This is, as Blessed John XXIII says, the *mystery* that lies at the heart of discernment.

Ignatius's teaching on discernment guides us to wise *human effort* in the sometimes long process of discernment, which may, in fact, include doubts and confusions along the way. As we make our best efforts, however, our confidence rests, finally, on the power of *God's grace* at work in our human efforts (1 Cor. 15:10).

LAURA says:

> When Steven and I got engaged, I had a moment of utter panic and doubt. I went to Steven and said, "How do we know that we will grow in the same direction? What if we go in completely different directions?" Steven said, "We don't know. That is fundamentally a question of whether we trust God. We know from experience what it was like to feel God's call. We have to trust that God will take care of that. It's a matter of faith."

STEVEN adds:

> This was a challenge. We had to put it on the line. I had to let Laura sort this out.

LAURA continues:

> After Steven said that, I told him that I needed a week to sort it out, but that I didn't want him to treat me differently during that time. It took me a couple of days. I rested on Steven's certitude. That's what pulled me through. I needed Steven's certitude, even when he didn't have an answer. He trusted God and the discernment. He didn't need to know the particulars of how it would work out.

Laura and Steven trust *God* and the *discernment*. The mystery of discernment is richly present in this blessed act of faith: human effort (*discernment*, that is, active involvement in the process, with its doubts and confusions along the way) and grace (*God*, that is, the outpouring of love and grace with which God accompanies the process) join together in a choice that Laura and Steven confidently identify as God's will for them.

DANIEL shares his experience:

After fifteen years with my company, things took a negative turn, and I could no longer accept some of the practices there. I began to consider starting my own company, but it was a big risk. I had a very good job, and to leave meant asking my family to run this risk with me. I was praying about this and talking to a priest, but I just wasn't sure.

When I spoke about this with my wife, Patricia, she said, "Let's pray, and do whatever God wants us to do, whether you need to stay or start a new business. You have to do what God wants you to do, and I'll support you." And she said, "We are in God's hands. I don't see why this should stop." She trusted that God would lead.

It was a hard process with times when, though I did everything I could, nothing seemed to be working. Finally, things changed and I began to see that the new business would work out. At that time, I was on a trip for the business. One morning I left the hotel and went to Mass in a church nearby. During the Mass I was looking at the Crucifix and I sensed God telling me that all this had happened

for a reason, "So that you will finally know and believe that
I love you."

Again the mystery of discernment is here: *human effort* ("I
was praying about this and talking to a priest. . . . I did everything I could") and *God's grace* (" 'We are in God's hands. . . .'
She trusted that God would lead"). That grace gives us courage
to make our best effort to discern, and sure hope that God will
guide that effort.

Chapter Nine

The Fruit of Discernment

Then the hand of the Lord came over St. Francis. As soon as he heard this answer and thereby knew the will of Christ, he got to his feet, all aflame with divine power, and said to Brother Masseo with great fervor: "So let us go — in the name of the Lord!" — From the *Fioretti* of St. Francis

"And This Gives Me Peace and Joy"

A few blocks from the residence where I lived as a seminarian was an elementary school run by a community of sisters. Our priests, and I with them after ordination, used to say Mass for the school. These same sisters worked in Africa, in hospitals and in education. In 1995, one of them, Sister Floralba, came briefly to the attention of the world.

Sister Floralba was born in 1924, in Pedrengo, a small city in northern Italy. When she was fifteen, her mother died and, for the next five years, she became a second mother to her younger brothers and sisters. She entered religious life when she was twenty, with a desire to serve in the missions.

Sister Floralba trained as a nurse with a specialization in tropical illnesses and spent forty-three years in the hospitals of

135

Africa. When she had served for twenty-five years in the hospital of Kikwit, in Zaire, she was sent back to Italy, where she expected to pass the remaining years of her life.

At the age of seventy-one, however, her superior asked her to return to the hospital in Kikwit. Sister Floralba said yes. Shortly after her return to Kikwit, she wrote to her superior:

> Forgive me if I haven't written earlier, but I wasn't ready; I wanted to wait for a short while. Having spent so many years in Kikwit, when I arrived I had the feeling of having always been here. . . . When I visited the hospital, I felt again all the demands of the work. . . . Yet I said to myself: I did not ask to come here, rather, I never thought they would send me here again since I had been here for twenty-five years. So I am sure that I am in the will of God, and this gives me peace and joy. I try to be with the sick and to help those who are especially ill. Since I have less work, I am trying to be more patient, more kind, more gentle with all. I want in the few years that remain to me to witness to the goodness and merciful love of the Father.[1]

Not long after, in April of 1995, Sister Floralba assisted a woman who underwent an operation in the hospital of Kikwit. Shortly thereafter, Sister Floralba fell ill, and on April 25, she died. She was the first of six sisters who would heroically give their lives in the outbreak of the Ebola virus in Zaire.

"So I am sure that I am in the will of God, and this gives me peace and joy": this unshakeable peace and joy, the certitude of being "in the will of God" that gives strength to love in even the most unexpected and humanly troubling circumstances of life — this is the fruit of discernment.

"In Your Will Is Our Peace"

We will listen a final time, now, as those who have discerned share the fruit of their discernment. **KATHLEEN** remembers the months before her marriage to Mark:

> I had thought about religious life briefly in high school, but never seriously. When Mark and I got engaged, the thought came back. I asked Mark for time to deal with this, and he lovingly gave it. We still saw each other, but less, and I had more time for silence and prayer. The whole discernment took two or three months. The Lord gave me a really beautiful gift and showed me clearly that he had made me for marriage with Mark.
>
> I came out of that time with absolute serenity about marrying Mark. I know how important that experience has been over the years. Times of struggle come, and I think, "I'm not a good mother," and so on, that I made a mistake. Then I remember that time when I knew that I was supposed to get married, and to Mark, and I can get on with handling the problem. I can think of how off-track I could have been without that discernment. I think it changes everything.
>
> There have been bumps along the road, but because there was that peace and serenity we could cope with them and keep going. We have been married for thirty years and have three children.

For Kathleen, discernment has been the bedrock of her life. In all the struggles of marriage and motherhood, the memory of her months of discernment supports her: "Then I remember that time when I knew that I was supposed to get married, and to Mark, and I can get on with handling the problem." The blessings of discernment are inexhaustible for Kathleen and Mark.

In chapter 3, we heard Matthew tell of his discernment regarding further studies. In fact, his religious superior asked Matthew to undertake those studies. As he recalls those years of study, MATTHEW adds:

> When I was doing the studies, it was very helpful to me to return to the origin of this discernment, that I wasn't looking for this, that it came from prayer. It helped me to decide the details of the studies. My heart's emphasis was on receiving this gift from God rather than as something that I was doing, just as the original idea was received from God.
>
> So the manner of the discernment became a manner of living the studies. I would go back to the discernment to keep me on this path. I would try to pray before I read, knowing that I had to receive this from God. It gave me confidence in continuing. There was a deepening through it in my relationship with God and my identity as a religious priest.

In Matthew's experience, the discernment becomes *a way of living* the choice that emerged from the process. The grace of the discernment is not simply a clarity in the past, but a gift that *shapes the entire living* of the choice. The ongoing blessings of his discernment process are evident: "It gave me *confidence* in continuing. There was a *deepening* through it in my *relationship with God* and my *identity* as a religious priest."

For years **JULIE** and **CARL** have discerned together the many decisions of their married life. Julie shares what such discernment means in their lives:

> Carl and I are individuals, but we are one. Our discernment is not so much in our individual walks, but in the marriage. There is a grace in it — we are both on the same path, equally yoked, joined in our prayer walk, so that we desire the same thing. We can talk about our prayer experiences freely because we both share this prayer in our lives. What Carl says often confirms and affirms my prayer, what is coming up in my prayer, and I do this for him. We keep each other accountable in prayer and encourage each other.

Clearly, discernment profoundly blesses this marriage: "We are both on the same path ... we desire the same thing." Here discernment has become an *ongoing way of life* which joins husband and wife in a common response to God's will.

PATRICK concludes his story with this simple and rich reflection on discernment:

> It's so great to be able to discern when you're not sure which way to go, when your heart is pulled in different ways and you don't see clearly with your thoughts. It's so

good to be able to bring this to the Lord, to a process of discernment, and to search for the answer.

Yes, it is a great blessing at such times — "when your heart is pulled in different ways and you don't see clearly with your thoughts ... to be able to bring this to the Lord, to a process of discernment." At such times, Ignatius's clear and practical teaching on discernment is an invaluable gift.

As I read Sister Floralba's letter and listen to Kathleen, Matthew, Julie, and Patrick, and as I ponder the many stories of discernment told in this book, I think of the words of St. Gregory Nazianzen so loved by Blessed John XXIII: "Voluntas tua pax nostra" — "In your will is our peace." Every story shared in this book reflects the truth of those words. The fruit of discernment — the process of finding the will of God — is, most deeply, the peace for which every human heart longs. That path lies open to us all.

Appendix

Complete Text of St. Ignatius[1]

[175] Three Times in Which a Sound and Good Choice May Be Made

The first time is when God Our Lord so moves and attracts the will that, without doubting or being able to doubt, the devout soul follows what is shown to it, as St. Paul and St. Matthew did in following Christ our Lord.

[176] *The second time* is when sufficient clarity and understanding is received through experience of consolations and desolations, and through experience of discernment of different spirits.

[177] *The third time* is one of tranquility, when one considers first for what purpose man is born, that is, to praise God our Lord and save his soul, and, desiring this, chooses as a means to this end some life or state within the bounds of the Church, so that he may be helped in the service of his Lord and the salvation of his soul. I said a tranquil time, that is, when the soul is not agitated by different spirits, and uses its natural powers freely and tranquilly.

[178] If the choice is not made in the first or second time, two ways of making it in this third time are given below.

The First Way to Make a Sound and Good Choice Contains Six Points

First Point. The first point is to place before myself the thing about which I wish to make a choice, such as an office or benefice[2] to be accepted or refused, or any other thing that may be the object of a choice that can be changed.[3]

[179] *Second Point.* The second. It is necessary to have as my objective the end for which I am created, that is, to praise God our Lord and save my soul. In addition, I must be indifferent, without any disordered attachment, so that I am not more inclined or disposed to accept the thing before me than to refuse it, nor to refuse it rather than accept it, but that I find myself like a balance at equilibrium, ready to follow whatever I perceive to be more for the glory and praise of God our Lord and the salvation of my soul.

[180] *Third Point.* The third. To ask God our Lord that he be pleased to move my will and place in my soul what I ought to do in the matter before me that would be more for his praise and glory, using my intellect well and faithfully to weigh the matter, and choosing in accord with what is pleasing to his most holy will.

[181] *Fourth Point.* The fourth. To consider by way of reasoning how many advantages or benefits accrue to me if I have the office or benefice proposed, solely for the praise of God our Lord and the salvation of my soul; and, on the contrary, to consider in the same way the disadvantages and dangers there would be in having it. Then to do the same in the second part,

that is, to look at the advantages and benefits in not having it, and, in the same way, at the disadvantages and dangers in not having it.

[182] *Fifth Point.* The fifth. After I have thought and reasoned in this way about every aspect of the matter before me, I will look to see toward which alternative reason inclines more; and, in this way, according to the greater movement of reason, and not through any sensual inclination, I should come to a decision in the matter under deliberation.

[183] *Sixth Point.* The sixth. Having made this choice or decision, the person who has made it should, with much diligence, turn to prayer before God our Lord and offer him this choice, so that his Divine Majesty may be pleased to receive and confirm it, if it is for his greater service and praise.

[184] The Second Way to Make a Sound and Good Choice Contains Four Rules and a Note

First Rule. The first is, that the love which moves me and causes me to choose this thing must descend from above, from the love of God; so that the one who chooses should first of all feel in himself that the love, greater or lesser, that he has for the thing he chooses, is solely for the sake of his Creator and Lord.

[185] *Second Rule.* The second, to look at a man whom I have never seen or known, and, desiring all perfection for him, consider what I would tell him to do and choose for the greater glory of God our Lord and the greater perfection of his soul;

and, doing myself the same, follow the rule that I propose to the other.

[186] *Third Rule.* The third, to consider, as if I were at the point of death, what procedure and norm of action I would then wish to have followed in making the present choice; and, guiding myself by this, make my decision entirely in conformity with it.

[187] *Fourth Rule.* The fourth, looking and considering how I will find myself on the day of judgment, to think of what decision I would then wish to have made about the present matter; and to adopt now the rule that I would then wish to have followed, so that then I may find myself in full satisfaction and joy.

[188] *Note.* Guided by the rules given above for my salvation and eternal peace, I will make my choice and my offering to God our Lord, in accordance with the sixth point of the first way of making a choice.

Notes

Introduction

1. My aim in this book, therefore, is clarity and usability. Consequently, I do not offer an exhaustive discussion of scholarly issues and specialized pastoral matters related to Ignatian discernment. Such a discussion, appropriate and valuable in another setting, would not serve the purpose of this book. Readers interested in such questions will find appropriate references in these endnotes, particularly in Part Two. My hope is to discuss these further issues in another book.

2. *The Discernment of Spirits: An Ignatian Guide for Everyday Living* (New York: Crossroad, 2005), and *Spiritual Consolation: An Ignatian Guide for the Greater Discernment of Spirits* (New York: Crossroad, 2007). Each book examines one of Ignatius's two sets of rules for the discernment of spirits.

3. See Jules Toner, S.J., *A Commentary on Saint Ignatius' Rules for the Discernment of Spirits: A Guide to the Principles and Practice* (St. Louis: Institute of Jesuit Sources, 1982), 12–15.

4. Written sources are acknowledged in the notes. The absence of a written source indicates that the quote is taken from an interview with the author.

Chapter 1: The Question

1. Ignatius clarifies these matters in *SpirEx*, 170–74.

2. Although Ignatius's teaching may be broadly applied, his primary concern in the Spiritual Exercises is choices of some relevance: one's vocation, or significant choices within that vocation. I adhere to this same criterion throughout this book. With regard to following God's will in the many small choices of daily living, Rainero Cantalamessa writes that, when I must decide "to make or not make a journey, to do a job, to make a visit, to buy something... I'll first

ask [God] by the simple means of prayer that is at everyone's dis-
posal, if it is his will that I make that journey, do that job, make that
visit, buy that object, and then I'll act or not.... I have submitted
the question to God. I have emptied myself of my own will. I have
renounced deciding for myself and I have given God the chance to
intervene in my life if he so wishes.... Just as a faithful servant never
takes an order from an outsider without saying, 'I must first ask my
master,' so the true servant of God undertakes nothing without saying
to himself, 'I must first pray a little to know what my Lord wants of
me!' The will of God thus penetrates one's existence more and more,
making it more precious and rendering it a 'living sacrifice, holy and
acceptable to God' (Rom. 12:1)." *Obedience: The Authority of the
Word* (Boston: St. Paul Books and Media, 1989), 56–57.

Chapter 2: The Foundation

1. Michael Scanlan, T.O.R., *What Does God Want? A Practical Guide to Making Decisions* (Steubenville, Ohio: Franciscan
University Press, 1996), 91.

2. Robert DeGrandis, S.S.J., compiler, and Linda Schubert, ed.,
*Renewed by the Holy Spirit: Testimonies of Priests Touched by the
Holy Spirit,* 3rd printing (1987), 2–3.

3. Ignatius describes these truths in *SpirEx,* 23, the "principle
and foundation" upon which our search for God's will is based.

4. *Vocation in Black and White: Dominican Contemplative
Nuns Tell How God Called Them* (Lincoln, Neb.: iUniverse, Inc.,
2008), 65–66. No name is given in the account, and I have supplied
the name "Catherine."

5. With good will, but without spiritual formation, Christopher
immediately equates discovery of God with a calling to priesthood.
Christopher wisely shares his thoughts with a priest, who assists him
to discern more fully. We will return to these questions in chapter 4.

6. Robert Baram, ed., *Spiritual Journeys: Twenty-seven Men and
Women Share Their Faith Experiences* (Boston: St. Paul Books and
Media, 1988), 168, 170.

7. John Henry Newman, *Meditations and Devotions* (London:
Longmans, Green and Co., 1925), 5. Emphasis added.

Chapter 3: The Disposition

1. Ignatius's word is the adjective "indiferente," which signifies precisely the freedom exemplified in Catherine's account. See *SpirEx*, 23, 157, 179.

2. Christine Mugridge and Jerry Usher, eds., *Called by Name: The Inspiring Stories of 12 Men Who Became Catholic Priests* (West Chester, Pa.: Ascension Press, 2008), 82–83.

3. For these spiritual means, see chapter 4.

4. As we will see in chapter 8, the struggles themselves involved in discernment have meaning in God's providential love.

5. The vow of poverty taken by the Jesuits and all religious priests.

6. Richard Hauser, S.J., *Moving in the Spirit: Becoming a Contemplative in Action* (Mahwah: N.J.: Paulist Press, 1986), 65, 67, 77–78. Ignatius describes Richard's disposition at this point — "I wanted to know God's will only if it confirmed my initial inclination" — in *SpirEx*, 154.

7. In the Spiritual Exercises, this is the movement from the Principle and Foundation (*SpirEx*, 23) to the meditations of the First Week (*SpirEx*, 45–72).

8. "The dynamic of the Spiritual Exercises, beginning with the first principle and foundation [*SpirEx*, 23], brings the retreatant first to look at God and, only then, at sin in the light of God. To know myself as a sinner is to grow in the knowledge of the loving, faithful God. Thus, I can look head on at my sinfulness, knowing that I am a loved sinner." Marian Cowan, C.S.J., and John Futrell, S.J., *Companions in Grace: Directing the Spiritual Exercises of St. Ignatius of Loyola* (St. Louis: Institute of Jesuit Sources, 2000), 41. Of this stage of the Spiritual Exercises, William Barry, S.J., writes: "A profound experience of the forgiveness of God and of the overwhelming realization that Jesus died for me, a sinner, leads to a great sense of freedom, a feeling that a weight has been lifted from one's heart and soul. There wells up in many people a spontaneous desire to return the favor, as it were, to get to know this Jesus who has so loved us and all human beings and suffered for me and for us." *Finding God*

in All Things: A Companion to the Spiritual Exercises of St. Ignatius (Notre Dame, Ind.: Ave Maria Press, 1991), 53.

9. *Priest Vocation Stories* (Lansing, Mich.: Faith Publishing Service, n.d.), 6.

10. This is the focus of his First Week in the Spiritual Exercises.

11. Mugridge and Usher, *Called by Name,* 179–80. Here I have changed the speaker's name to "Thomas."

12. Translation from Timothy Gallagher, O.M.V., *The Discernment of Spirits: An Ignatian Guide to Everyday Living* (New York: Crossroad, 2005), 7. Emphasis added.

13. Rite of Christian Initiation of Adults. Arthur teaches the classes that prepare adult candidates to enter the Catholic Church.

14. *Priest Vocation Stories,* 12.

15. This is the primary focus of the Second Week, the longest of the four, in the Spiritual Exercises. In this Second Week, Ignatius emphasizes the humility and poverty of Christ (*SpirEx,* 98, 116, 143–47, 167), and invites those discerning to seek such dispositions in prayer. For Ignatius, the heart grows in readiness to discern as it increasingly embraces Christ's own humility and love of poverty. See Candido de Dalmases, S.J., *Ignatius of Loyola, Founder of the Jesuits: His Life and Work* (St. Louis: Institute of Jesuit Sources, 1985), 68–69; Jules Toner, S.J., *Discerning God's Will: Ignatius of Loyola's Teaching on Christian Decision Making* (St. Louis: Institute of Jesuit Sources, 1991), 87–95.

16. Thomas of Celano, *First Life,* 115, in Marion Habig, ed., *St. Francis of Assisi: Writings and Early Biographies. English Omnibus of the Sources for the Life of St. Francis* (Quincy, Ill.: Franciscan Press, 1991), 329. Emphasis in the original.

Chapter 4: The Means

1. *SpirEx,* 20, 72, 128, 129ff. See also his *Spiritual Diary,* in which daily Mass lies at the heart of his discernment.

2. Association of the Monasteries of Nuns of the Order of Preachers of the United States of America, *Vocation in Black and White: Dominican Contemplative Nuns Tell How God Called Them* (Lincoln, Neb.: iUniverse, 2008), 33–34.

3. Weeks Two, Three, and Four in the Spiritual Exercises are dedicated primarily to contemplation of Jesus in the Gospels.

4. For this approach to prayer, see Timothy Gallagher, O.M.V., *Meditation and Contemplation: An Ignatian Guide to Praying with Scripture* (New York: Crossroad, 2008), and *An Ignatian Introduction to Prayer: Scriptural Reflections according to the* Spiritual Exercises (New York: Crossroad, 2008). Ignatius employs both meditation (reflective approach) and contemplation (imaginative approach) in the Spiritual Exercises, though more frequently the latter.

5. Gallagher, *Meditation and Contemplation*, 38–39.

6. Ibid., 42.

7. Kierkegaard writes: "If I were a physician and someone asked me 'What do you think should be done?' I would answer, 'The first thing, the unconditional condition for anything to be done is: create silence, bring about silence; God's Word cannot be heard, and if in order to be heard in the hullabaloo it must be shouted deafeningly with noisy instruments, then it is not God's Word; create silence!" Howard Hong and Edna Hong, eds. and trans., Søren Kierkegaard, *For Self Examination/Judge for Yourself* (Princeton, N.J.: Princeton University Press, 1990), 47.

8. Rite of Christian Initiation for Adults. The program includes classes in the faith.

9. The person dedicates an hour to prayer each day and meets weekly with the retreat director. The process normally continues for several months. Such retreats are called the Exercises in Daily Life, or the Nineteenth Annotation Retreat (*SpirEx*, 19).

10. Michael Scanlan, T.O.R., *What Does God Want? A Practical Guide to Making Decisions* (Steubenville, Ohio: Franciscan University Press, 1996), 73.

11. See Gallagher, *Meditation and Contemplation*, 73–76, and *The Examen Prayer: Ignatian Wisdom for Our Lives Today* (New York: Crossroad, 2006), 132–35.

12. Gallagher, *Meditation and Contemplation*, 74.

13. Ibid., 75.

14. My treatment of the examen prayer here is brief only because I discuss this prayer at length in *The Examen Prayer.* Growth in the

examen prayer is invaluable for discernment and abundantly merits the attention of those who discern.

15. In addition to the means described, Ignatius also mentions general confession (*SpirEx*, 44), penance (*SpirEx*, 82–89), and spiritual reading (*SpirEx*, 100). The first suggests that the sacrament of reconciliation may also serve as an ongoing preparation for discernment. Ignatius describes both the fruits of penance (*SpirEx*, 87) and the means toward attaining wise balance in penitential practices (*SpirEx*, 89); here too spiritual guidance is beneficial. In accord with Ignatius's counsel, spiritual reading might include the Gospels, spiritual classics, and the lives of the saints. Those interviewed frequently mentioned the value of such reading in their discernment.

16. In Thomistic terms, this is the question of *judgment*, the second act of prudence, which follows upon *counsel* (deliberation) and prepares for *command* (effective decision to act). *Summa Theologiae*, IIa–IIae, q. 47, a. 8.

17. "I asked the pilgrim [St. Ignatius] about the Exercises, the Constitutions, wishing to learn how he drew them up. He answered that the Exercises were not composed all at one time, but things he had observed in his own soul and found useful, and which he thought would be useful to others, he put into writing — the examination of conscience, for example, with the idea of the lines of different length, and so on. The forms of the election [ways of discerning God's will] in particular, he told me, came from that variety of movement of spirits and thoughts which he experienced at Loyola, while he was convalescing from his shattered leg." William Young, S.J., trans., *St. Ignatius' Own Story: As Told to Luis González da Câmara* (Chicago: Henry Regnery Company, 1956), 69.

Chapter 5: Clarity beyond Doubting

1. *Autobiography*, no. 27. Author's translation. Ignatius related these events to Luis Gonçalves da Câmara, who later conserved them in writing. For this reason, da Câmara uses the third person singular ("he was," "he had").

2. Ignatius uses two words, *time* ("tiempo": *SpirEx*, 175–78; *Autograph Directory*, 6) and *mode* ("modo": *Autograph Directory*,

18–19), for the three ways of discerning God's will described in the Spiritual Exercises. In this book, I will use the second, "mode," as the more immediately accessible of the two.

3. Luis González Hernández, S.J., suggests that Ignatius's choice of the name "Company of Jesus" for his religious community, and his decision to recount the story of his life to Luis Gonçalves da Câmara may also have been discernments of this kind: *El primer tiempo de elección según San Ignacio* (Madrid: Ediciónes Studium, 1956), 25, n. 28.

4. Jules Toner highlights these three elements in *Discerning God's Will: Ignatius of Loyola's Teaching on Christian Decision Making* (St. Louis: Institute of Jesuit Sources, 1991), 109.

5. For this reason Ignatius calls this mode the *first* of the modes ("first time"). If God simply gives the gift of clarity in the choice, there is no need to proceed to the further modes of discernment — the second and third — which he describes immediately after the first. Experiences like that of Andrew quoted on pp. 74–76 indicate, however, that God may grant first-mode clarity at a given moment in a discernment already in process according to the second or third mode.

6. "The account given here is just as it was written by the person who had the experience. 'Malia' is a pseudonym." Toner, *Discerning God's Will*, 112, n. 14. Toner gives the account on pp. 112–13.

7. Sr. Margaret Mary of the Sacred Heart, "Vocation story," Passionist Nuns, St. Joseph Monastery, Whitesville, Kentucky. See at *www.passionistnuns.org/vocationstories/AVocationStory/index.htm*.

8. Christine Mugridge and Jerry Usher, eds., *Called by Name: The Inspiring Stories of 12 Men Who Became Catholic Priests* (West Chester, Pa.: Ascension Press, 2008), 180.

9. See n. 5 above. This is how I understand the moment before the altar described in the Introduction.

10. See Toner, *Discerning God's Will*, 118–21, and Luis González Hernández, S.J., *El primer tiempo de elección según San Ignacio* (Madrid: Ediciónes Studium, 1956), 109. Both books are excellent sources for further reading on first-mode discernment.

Chapter 6: An Attraction of the Heart

1. William Young, S.J., trans., in Simon Decloux, S.J., *Commentaries on the Letters and Spiritual Diary of St. Ignatius Loyola* (Rome: Centrum Ignatianum Spiritualitatis, 1980), 134–35. Further details regarding the question of poverty to be discerned and Ignatius's process of discernment are available in all editions of the *Spiritual Diary*. To simplify the reading, I have omitted Ignatius's indication of the specific Mass (Holy Trinity, Name of Jesus, Our Lady) he celebrated each day, and the translator's inclusion in brackets of the day of the month: February 3, etc.

2. In *SpirEx*, 147, Ignatius asks the intercession of Mary with her Son, and of the Son with the Father.

3. March 12, 1544. Author's translation, in *The Examen Prayer: Ignatian Wisdom for Our Lives Today* (New York: Crossroad, 2006), 46. The continuation of the quotation is from this same source. Unless otherwise indicated, all further quotations from Ignatius's writings are translated by the author.

4. In *SpirEx*, 176, Ignatius speaks both of the "experience of consolations and desolations" and of the "experience of discernment of different spirits." Does he understand these experiences as identical (a single experience formulated in different words) or as distinct (two different experiences, each sufficient for discernment, or complementary)? For this question, see José Calveras, S.J., "Buscar y hallar la voluntad divina por los tiempos de elección de los Ejercicios de S. Ignacio," *Manresa* 15 (1943): 259–64; and Daniel Gil, S.J., *Discernimiento según San Ignacio: Exposición y comentario práctico de las dos series de reglas de discernimiento de espíritus contenidas en el libro de los Ejercicios Espirituales de San Ignacio de Loyola*, EE 313–36 (Rome: Centrum Ignatianum Spiritualitatis, 1983), 16–18. Both authors, in different ways, see these two experiences as distinct.

5. *Autograph Directory*, 18.

6. In the Second Week of the Spiritual Exercises, the one discerning prays daily on the mysteries of Christ in the Gospels: *SpirEx*, 261–88. This suggests the value of such prayer in daily life for one seeking to discern by the second mode outside the retreat.

7. "Third Rule. The third is of spiritual consolation. I call it consolation when some interior movement is caused in the soul, through which the soul comes to be inflamed with love of its Creator and Lord, and, consequently when it can love no created thing on the face of the earth in itself, but only in the Creator of them all. Likewise when it sheds tears that move to love of its Lord, whether out of sorrow for one's sins, or for the passion of Christ our Lord, or because of other things directly ordered to his service and praise. Finally, I call consolation every increase of hope, faith and charity, and all interior joy that calls and attracts to heavenly things and to the salvation of one's soul, quieting it and giving it peace in its Creator and Lord" (*SpirEx*, 316). "*Fourth Rule*. The fourth is of spiritual desolation. I call desolation all the contrary of the third rule, such as darkness of soul, disturbance in it, movement to low and earthly things, disquiet from various agitations and temptations, moving to lack of confidence, without hope, without love, finding oneself totally slothful, tepid, sad and, as if separated from one's Creator and Lord. For just as consolation is contrary to desolation, in the same way the thoughts that come from consolation are contrary to the thoughts that come from desolation." (*SpirEx*, 317). Timothy Gallagher, *The Discernment of Spirits: An Ignatian Guide to Everyday Living* (New York: Crossroad, 2005), 7–8. I discuss spiritual consolation and spiritual desolation on pp. 47–71 of this book. Ignatius's counsel highlights the need for spiritual directors prepared to explain spiritual consolation and spiritual desolation to those who discern, and able to accompany them wisely in this sensitive mode of discernment.

8. Jules Toner brings together these three Ignatian texts (*SpirEx*, 176; *Autograph Directory*, 18; *SpirEx*, 318) in *Discerning God's Will: Ignatius of Loyola's Teaching on Christian Decision Making* (St. Louis: Institute of Jesuit Sources, 1991), 130–34.

9. "The second time is when *sufficient* ["asaz"] clarity and understanding is received through experience of consolations and desolations..." (*SpirEx*, 176). When is *sufficient* clarity and understanding for second-mode discernment present? On the meaning of "asaz," see Eusebio Hernández, S.J., "La elección en los Ejercicios de San Ignacio," *Miscelánea Comillas* 24 (1956): 133, n. 34; and Jules Toner, *Discerning God's Will*, 131, n. 2.

10. In this discussion of second-mode discernment, I have focused on the "experience of *consolation* and *desolation*" (*SpirEx*, 176), that is, on discernment according to the *First Set* of Rules for the discernment of spirits, when the good spirit counsels through spiritual *consolation* and the bad through spiritual *desolation*. Completeness of exposition would require a similar treatment of discernment according to the *Second Set* of Rules, when the bad spirit, disguised as an "angel of light," imitates the good spirit and counsels through (deceptive) spiritual *consolation*. Clearly, discernment according to the Second Set of Rules is crucial for those who face such deception. In this book, however, I think it best to follow Ignatius's counsel (*SpirEx*, 9) and not mix discussion of discernment according to the First Set of Rules with that of the Second Set. I have explored discernment according to the Second Set of Rules at length in *Spiritual Consolation: An Ignatian Guide for the Greater Discernment of Spirits* (New York: Crossroad, 2007), to which I refer the reader. As always — and perhaps above all in the "subtle and elevated" (*SpirEx*, 9) discernment of spirits described in the Second Set of Rules — Ignatius presumes accompaniment by a spiritual guide.

11. As we will see in the following chapter, Ignatius discerns simultaneously according to the second and third modes, both of which lead him to the same conclusion.

12. Richard Hauser, S.J., *Moving in the Spirit: Becoming a Contemplative in Action* (Mahwah, N.J.: Paulist Press, 1986), 75–76, 79.

13. Association of the Monasteries of Nuns of the Order of Preachers of the United States of America, *Vocation in Black and White: Dominican Contemplative Nuns Tell How God Called Them* (Lincoln, Neb.: iUniverse, 2008), 24–25.

14. Maria says of this conversation that "he encouraged me to follow whatever God was asking." This is precisely the question Maria faces: What is God asking? In fact, many years pass before Maria concludes her discernment. Ignatius's teaching is an invaluable resource for spiritual directors in discernments of this kind.

15. Very probably they are, though Maria's vocabulary does not express this clearly. On the distinction between *spiritual* and *nonspiritual* consolation and desolation, see Gallagher, *The Discernment of Spirits*, 48–51, 60–61.

16. See ibid., 18–20, and *The Examen Prayer*, 137–47.

17. See chapter 2, p. 26 above.

18. See n. 7 on p. 153.

19. I have discussed discernment of spirits in two books: *The Discernment of Spirits* (First Set of Rules) and *Spiritual Consolation* (Second Set of Rules). Space does not allow me to repeat here all that is said in these books. I refer the reader to them, therefore, for that deeper understanding of discernment of spirits so essential for second-mode discernment. Of the two, the first, *The Discernment of Spirits*, is the more fundamental.

20. Commentators on second-mode discernment suggest two general ways of approaching this discernment. In the first, we attentively *wait to see* if God gives a consistent attraction to one option in time of spiritual consolation (or if we experience the contrary in spiritual desolation). In the second, we *propose* one or the other option to God and attentively note the response of our hearts. This second, more active approach to second-mode discernment may be done in various ways: Eusebio Hernández, S.J., "La elección en los Ejercicios de San Ignacio," *Miscelánea Comillas* 24 (1956): 137–40; Jacinto Ayerra, S.J., "Psicología del Segundo Tiempo," *Miscelánea Comillas* 33 (1959): 284–87; Martin Palmer, S.J., ed. and trans., *On Giving the Spiritual Exercises: The Early Jesuit Manuscript Directories and the Official Directory of 1599* (St. Louis: Institute of Jesuit Sources, 1996), 9 [21], 256–57 [122–28], 336 [220], etc. As noted, Ignatius always presumes the assistance of a knowledgeable guide in such discernment. On the early Jesuit Directories and their understanding of second-mode discernment, see Alfredo Sampaio, S.J., *Los tiempos de elección en los directories de Ejercicios* (Bilbao: Mensajero, Sal Terrae, 2004), 133–46.

21. José Calveras, S.J., writes: "Let no one assume, then, from all that we have said about this [second-mode] time that any movement, sentiment, or interior impulse may be taken as a sign of God's will,

and, even less, that it may be followed and put into practice, without subjecting it to a diligent exam according to the rules for discernment of spirits, and without speaking about the matter with another, if it is a matter of some importance": "Buscar y hallar la voluntad divina por los tiempos de elección de los Ejercicios de S. Ignacio," *Manresa* 15 (1943): 264.

22. A further question regards whether Ignatius expects one who discerns according to the second mode to seek *confirmation* from God of this discernment, after the choice is (tentatively) made. Ignatius explicitly asks for such confirmation in the third mode of discerning (*SpirEx*, 183, 188); he does not mention this, however, with respect to the second mode. Jules Toner, basing himself on Ignatius's own practice in his *Spiritual Diary,* argues that Ignatius does expect those who discern according to the second mode to seek confirmation after reaching a tentative conclusion: *Discerning God's Will,* 159–60, 202. Because Ignatius speaks of such confirmation in reference to third-mode discernment, I will discuss it in the next chapter rather than this. Everything said about confirmation there may be applied to second-mode discernment as well. See also "Concluding the Process" in chapter 8. For an approach to confirmation in second-mode discernment, see Eusebio Hernández, S.J., "La elección en los Ejercicios de San Ignacio," *Miscelánea Comillas* 24 (1956): 142–43.

Chapter 7: A Preponderance of Reasons

1. See Joseph Munitiz, S.J., and Philip Endean, S.J., eds. and trans., *Saint Ignatius of Loyola: Personal Writings* (London: Penguin Books, 1996), 70–72.

2. Ibid., 70.

3. *SpirEx*, 178; *Autograph Directory,* 19. As Ignatius's example shows, the second and third mode of discernment may be combined. In fact, in his discernment between radical and mitigated poverty, Ignatius simultaneously employs the second and the third modes of discernment: he simultaneously notes experiences of spiritual consolation and desolation and the inclination he feels at such times with respect to either option (second mode), and reviews the reasons that suggest that either option may be for God's greater glory (third

mode). Both modes lead him to discern that God wills him to choose radical poverty.

4. "By 'natural powers' in this context, Ignatius surely means those powers used in the third mode of discerning God's will: insight, reason, imagination, memory, and will (firmly set on the greater glory [of God] and on finding the significant facts and reasoning correctly). By 'free and tranquil use' of these powers, he means their unimpeded and undisturbed functioning in searching out and arguing the advantages and disadvantages of alternatives for God's service." Jules Toner, *Discerning God's Will: Ignatius of Loyola's Teaching on Christian Decision Making* (St. Louis: Institute of Jesuit Sources, 1991), 167.

5. Pedro de Ribadeneyra, *Vita Ignatii Loyolae,* Monumenta Historica Societatis Iesu, 93, 739–41.

6. For Ignatius's complete text, see the Appendix, *SpirEx,* 178–83.

7. See Toner, *Discerning God's Will,* 173–75.

8. This is sometimes described as the method of the four columns: the advantages and disadvantages of the first, and then of the second option. For a further example of this method, see Martin Palmer, S.J., *On Giving the Spiritual Exercises: The Early Jesuit Manuscript Directories and the Official Directory of 1599* (St. Louis: Institute of Jesuit Sources, 1996), 352–56.

9. *Spiritual Diary,* February 8, 1544. Further steps in the discernment will confirm Ignatius, not without struggle, in this judgment.

10. Clearly, the one discerning is to consider the weight of the various advantages and disadvantages, and not only their number.

11. Patrick's experience raises the question of spiritual direction by a family member. In this instance, the process works well. Care is necessary, however, in any double relationship of this nature (family relationship, relationship of spiritual direction). The mingling of the two is most often not advisable.

12. *Autograph Directory,* 19–20.

13. Toner, *Discerning God's Will,* 182–89; Calveras, "Buscar y hallar la voluntad divina por los tiempos de elección de los Ejercicios de S. Ignacio," *Manresa* 15 (1943): 267–68; Hernández, "La elección

en los Ejercicios de San Ignacio," *Miscelánea Comillas* 24 (1956): 148–52.

14. For Ignatius's complete text, see the Appendix, *SpirEx,* 184–88.

15. Toner makes this point in *Discerning God's Will,* 187.

16. Ignatius proposes these three same tests in his Rules for Almsgiving, *SpirEx,* 339–41.

17. As indicated, we will discuss confirmation further in the next chapter.

Chapter 8: The Value of the Process of Discernment

1. *Spiritual Diary,* February 8, 1544. Although Ignatius does conclude with the choice for radical poverty, he will continue to seek confirmation until March 12.

2. This paragraph follows Jules Toner's summary of Ignatius's experiences of confirmation in *Discerning God's Will: Ignatius of Loyola's Teaching on Christian Decision Making* (St. Louis: Institute of Jesuit Sources, 1991), 210.

3. Association of the Monasteries of Nuns of the Order of Preachers of the United States of America, *Vocations in Black and White: Dominican Contemplative Nuns Tell How God Called Them* (Lincoln, Neb.: iUniverse, 2008), 26.

4. Christine Mugridge and Jerry Usher, eds., *Called by Name: The Inspiring Stories of 12 Men Who Became Catholic Priests* (West Chester, Pa.: Ascension Press, 2008), 110.

5. In this book we have focused on the *spiritual* disposition necessary for fruitful discernment (chapter 3). Because the spiritual presupposes and builds on the human, however, the *human* disposition (psychological maturity) is also critically important in discernment. Struggles in discernment may arise from such human issues, and many obstacles in discernment are resolved when those discerning and their guides attend to such issues, should they be present. See Laurence Murphy, S.J., "Psychological Problems of Christian Choice," *The Way Supplement* 24 (1975): 26–35.

6. James Martin, S.J., *Becoming Who You Are: Insights on the True Self from Thomas Merton and Other Saints* (Mahwah, N.J.: Hidden Spring, 2006), 17.

Chapter 9: The Fruit of Discernment

1. From a newsletter of the Sisters of the Poverelle.

Appendix

1. Author's translation from the Spanish Autograph version, in *Monumenta Historica Societatis Iesu,* 100, 262–76. My translation adheres to Ignatius's own Spanish, with limited adaptations as necessary for comprehensible reading in English. The vocabulary and occasional awkwardness of wording in the translation reflect the original. In translating, I have consulted and at various points adopted wording from other translations, in particular, Louis Puhl, S.J., *The Spiritual Exercises of St. Ignatius: Based on Studies in the Language of the Autograph* (Chicago: Loyola University Press, 1951), and Michael Ivens, S.J., *Understanding the Spiritual Exercises: Text and Commentary: A Handbook for Retreat Directors* (Leominster: Gracewing, Inigo Enterprises, 1998). "Complete" in the title to this Appendix signifies Ignatius's full text with regard to the three modes of discernment (*SpirEx,* 175–88). Ignatius also discusses the "election," that is, discerning God's will, in *SpirEx,* 135, 169–74, 189. The numbers in brackets are added to the original; they are standard usage in citing the paragraphs of the *Spiritual Exercises.*

2. In Ignatius's time, a position of ministry granted to members of the clergy that also provided financial support.

3. "There are matters that fall under an unchangeable choice, such as priesthood, marriage, etc. There are others that fall under a changeable choice, such as to accept or relinquish benefices, or to acquire or renounce temporal goods." *SpirEx,* 171.

Which Ignatian title is right for you?

Tens of thousands of readers are turning to Fr. Gallagher's Ignatian titles for reliable, inspirational, and clear explanations of some of the most important aspects of Christian spirituality. Whether you're a spiritual director, priest or minister, longtime spiritual seeker, or beginner, Fr. Gallagher's books have much to offer you in different moments in life.

When you need short, practical exercises for young and old:
An Ignatian Introduction to Prayer

Group leaders who are looking for practical exercises for groups, including groups who may not have much experience in spiritual development, will want to acquire *An Ignatian Introduction to Prayer: Scriptural Reflections According to the Spiritual Exercises*. This book features forty short (two-page) Ignatian meditations, including scripture passages, meditative keys for entering into the scriptural story, and guided questions for reflection. These exercises are also useful for individual reflection both for experienced persons and beginners: beginners will recognize and resonate with some of the evocative passages from scripture; those familiar with Ignatian teaching will appreciate the Ignatian structure of the guided questions.

When your life is at a crossroads:
Discerning the Will of God

If you are facing a turning point in life, you know how difficult it can be to try to hear God's will amid the noise of other people's expectations and your own wishes. Ignatius of Loyola developed a series of exercises and reflections designed to help you in these times so that your decision can be one that conforms to God's will for your life.

Discerning the Will of God: An Ignatian Guide to Christian Decision Making is a trustworthy guide to applying those reflections to your own particular circumstances. This guide, which does not require any prior knowledge of Ignatian spirituality, can be used by people of any faith, though some elements will be more directly applicable to Catholic readers.

When you want classic spiritual discipline to apply every day: *The Examen Prayer* and *Meditation and Contemplation*

Individuals wanting to deepen their prayer lives using a spiritual discipline will find *The Examen Prayer* an important resource. The examen prayer is a powerful and increasingly popular practice for finding God's hand in our everyday lives and learning to be receptive to God's blessings. This easy-to-read book uses stories and examples to explain what the examen is, how you can begin to pray it, how you can adapt it to your individual life, and what its benefits for your life can be. Highly practical!

A second favorite is *Meditation and Contemplation: An Ignatian Guide to Praying with Scripture*. Anyone familiar with Ignatian spirituality has heard about meditation and contemplation. In this volume, Fr. Gallagher explains what is unique to each practice, shows how you can profit from both at different times in your spiritual life, and reveals some of the forgotten elements (such as the preparatory steps and colloquy) and how the structure can be adapted to your particular spiritual needs.

Because *The Examen Prayer* draws from the experiences of everyday life, it can stand on its own as a guide to the prayer of examen. Those looking to begin their practice of meditation and contemplation, which for Ignatius is always based on scripture, may choose their own scripture passages or draw from the forty examples in *An Ignatian Introduction to Prayer*, mentioned earlier.

When you're ready to move more deeply into Ignatian thought: *The Discernment of Spirits* **and** *Spiritual Consolation*

Spiritual directors, directees, and others who want to understand the deeper structures of Ignatian thought have come to rely on *The Discernment of Spirits: An Ignatian Guide to Everyday Living*, and *Spiritual Consolation: An Ignatian Guide for the Greater Discernment of Spirits*. *The Discernment of Spirits* leads us through Ignatius's Rules for discernment, showing both their precise insight into the human soul and their ability to illustrate the real-life struggles of spiritual seekers today. As Fr. Gallagher writes, his practical goal is "to offer an experience-based presentation of Ignatius's rules for discernment of spirits in order to facilitate their ongoing application in the spiritual life. This is a book about living the spiritual life." Because it forms the foundation for so many other aspects of Ignatian thought, *The Discernment of Spirits* has become Fr. Gallagher's bestselling book and has been the basis for a TV series.

Spiritual Consolation extends this same approach, interweaving stories and principles for a more profound understanding of Ignatius's Second Rules for discernment.